Tragedies and Mysteries of Rock 'n' Roll

METRO BOOKS
New York

TEXT BY

MICHELE PRIMI

project editor
VALERIA MANFERTO DE FABIANIS

graphic design
MARINELLA DEBERNARDI

editorial staff
GIADA FRANCIA - GIORGIA RAINERI - FRANCESCA PISCITELLO

editorial consulting
MARCO DE FABIANIS MANFERTO

Contents

Stories of the
ROCK CURSE

"WE'RE GOING TO LIVE, OR WE'RE GOING TO DIE. IF WE'RE DEAD, WE'RE GOING TO HAVE TO DEAL WITH THAT. IF WE'RE ALIVE, WE'RE GOING TO HAVE TO DEAL WITH BEING ALIVE." THAT WAS HOW JOHN LENNON SUMMED UP THE RELATIONSHIP BETWEEN ROCK ARTISTS AND LIFE. THOSE WERE THE WORDS OF A GENIUS WHO DEMONSTRATED, MORE THAN ANY OTHER, THAT MUSIC, LIKE EVERY ART FORM, LIVES ON EVEN AFTER DEATH.

EVEN AFTER FOUR SHOTS FIRED BY A DERANGED PERSON WHO WANTED TO ACHIEVE FAME AND IMMORTALITY BY MURDERING THE GREATEST ROCK STAR ON EARTH BUT ONLY ENDED UP IN THE OBLIVION OF THOSE WHO ARE GUILTY OF HAVING DEPRIVED THE WORLD OF THE CHANCE TO DISCOVER NEW FORMS OF CREATIVITY.

THIS VOLUME RELATES 63 STORIES OF ART, LIFE AND DEATH IN THE ROCK 'N' ROLL WORLD. STORIES OF LIVES CUT SHORT AT THE HEIGHT OF THEIR CREATIVITY, OF INCREDIBLE ENCOUNTERS WITH FATE, AND OF ARTISTS WHO DIED AFTER YEARS OF STRUGGLE AGAINST THEIR DEMONS, WHICH WERE BECOMING MORE AND MORE OPPRESSIVE AND DIFFICULT TO DEAL WITH. THEY RANGE FROM BUDDY HOLLY TO WHITNEY HOUSTON, MUSICAL LEGENDS WHO LIVED IN DIFFERENT PERIODS AND ALSO DIFFERED IN THEIR LIFESTYLES AND WAYS OF EXPRESSING THEIR TALENT, BUT WERE SIMILAR IN THAT THEY WERE ICONS OF OUR TIME.

MANY OF THEM BELONG TO THE, SO-CALLED, 27 CLUB, A GROUP OF MUSICIANS AND SINGERS WHO ALL HAPPENED TO DIE AT THE AGE OF 27. THE FIRST WAS ROBERT JOHNSON, WHO DIED ON 16 AUGUST 1938, AND THE LAST WAS AMY WINEHOUSE, DIED ON 23 JULY 2011. THESE DISTURBING STATISTICS HAVE BECOME LEGENDARY. THE "CLUB" WAS "FOUNDED" IN THE EARLY 1970S, WHEN SOME OF THE KEY FIGURES OF THE MUSIC WORLD OF THE TIME – BRIAN JONES, JANIS JOPLIN, JIMI HENDRIX AND JIM MORRISON – DIED AT THE AGE OF 27, WITHIN THE SPACE OF A FEW YEARS. OTHER "MEMBERS" WERE ADDED: CELEBRITIES SUCH AS PETE DE FREITAS OF ECHO & THE BUNNYMEN, DAVE ALEXANDER OF THE STOOGES, IAN CURTIS OF JOY DIVISION, MIA ZAPATA OF THE GITS, KRISTEN PFAFF OF HOLE, JEAN MICHEL BASQUIAT OF GRAY AND FREAKY TAH OF THE LOST BOYZ. ON 1 FEBRUARY 1995, RICHEY EDWARDS OF THE MANIC STREET PREACHERS, DISAPPEARED WHEN HE WAS 27; HE WAS NEVER FOUND AND, IN 2008, WAS OFFICIALLY DECLARED DEAD. IS THIS ONLY A COINCIDENCE?

THE MASS MEDIA CREATED THE LEGEND. POPULAR

IMAGINATION WENT IN SEARCH OF MYSTERIOUS PLOTS ON THE PART OF THE FBI OR UNSCRUPULOUS MANAGERS AND PRODUCERS (SUCH AS MIKE JEFFERY, WHO WAS SUSPECTED OF RELATIONS WITH THE MAFIA AND THE BRITISH SECRET SERVICE AND ACCUSED BY MANY OF HAVING CAUSE THE DEATH OF JIMI HENDRIX IN ORDER TO POCKET A HUGE INSURANCE POLICY). INEVITABLY THE PUBLIC BECAME CURIOUS AND EXCITED AND TRANSFORMED THESE MUSICIANS INTO ICONS. EVEN THE SCIENTIFIC WORLD HAS TRIED TO PROVIDE AN ANSWER: A STUDY OF MORE THAN 1,000 CASES, CONDUCTED BY LIVERPOOL JOHN MOORES UNIVERSITY, HAS DEMONSTRATED THAT ROCK STARS HAVE TWICE THE PROBABILITY OF DYING YOUNG COMPARED WITH THE REST OF THE WORLD'S POPULATION.

IF ROCK 'N' ROLL IS A KEY TO AN INTERPRETATION OF THE CONTEMPORARY WORLD OF THE LAST 60 YEARS, THESE TRAGIC EVENTS TELL US QUITE A LOT ABOUT HOW IT HAS CHANGED. THE PIONEERS OF ROCK IN THE 1950S LOST THEIR LIVES IN CIRCUMSTANCES THAT WOULD HAVE BEEN AVOIDED TODAY; THOSE OF THE 1960S WERE OVERWHELMED BY DRUGS AND A RAMPANT LIFESTYLE; THE GENERATION OF THE LAST DECADE OF THE 20TH CENTURY AND THE FIRST DECADE OF THE 21ST CENTURY WAS SWALLOWED UP BY THE DARKNESS OF DESPAIR AND SOLITUDE. OTIS REDDING'S AIRPLANE, WHICH CRASHED DURING THE NIGHT AT MADISON, THE BOTTLE OF JOHN BONHAM AND BON SCOTT, HILLEL SLOVAK'S AND ANDREW WOOD'S SYRINGE, AND KURT COBAIN'S RIFLE – ARE ALL SYMBOLS OF A FREE, REBELLIOUS LIFESTYLE THAT WAS EXCESSIVE AND ON THE EDGE, WHICH OFTEN HAD TOO HIGH A PRICE. THEY ARE ALSO PART OF THE HISTORY OF ROCK 'N' ROLL.

DESCRIBING THE LIVES OF THESE MUSICIANS ALSO MEANS DISCOVERING THE REAL PEOPLE BEHIND THE STAGE PERSONAS, WITH ALL THEIR DOUBTS, IMPERFECTIONS AND CREATIVITY.

IT IS QUITE NORMAL TO BE ANGRY, BAFFLED AND SAD WHEN READING ABOUT YOUNG PEOPLE STRUCK DOWN BY AN IRREPRESSIBLE IMPULSE TO SELF-DESTRUCT, SUCH AS SID VICIOUS AND LAYNE STALEY, OR BY AN INCOMPREHENSIBLE DESTINY LIKE THE ONE THAT AWAITED JACO PASTORIUS, CLIFF BURTON AND JEFF BUCKLEY, THE MAN WITH AN ANGEL'S VOICE WHO DROWNED IN THE MISSISSIPPI AFTER HAVING RECORDED ONLY ONE ALBUM. HOW COULD IT HAVE BEEN OTHERWISE? THE BEST WAY TO OVERCOME THESE FEELINGS AND REACTIONS IS TO DISCOVER HOW MUCH ART AND LIFE EXISTED BEFORE THAT LAST, FATAL DAY, HOW MANY STEPS THERE WERE ON THE STAIRWAY THE LED THESE ARTISTS TOWARD ETERNITY.

AND DISCOVERING THIS IS PRECISELY THE REASON WHY THIS BOOK DEALS MOSTLY WITH THE LIFE OF THE ROCK STARS AND NOT ONLY THEIR DEATH, EVEN WHEN THE END WAS WRAPPED IN MYSTERY OR WAS LIKE SOMETHING ONE READS IN THE CRIME PAGES OF NEWSPAPERS, SUCH AS THE MURDERS OF DIMEBAG DARRELL, PETER TOSH AND JOHN LENNON. TAKEN AS A WHOLE, THESE CASES – SOME OF WHICH REMAIN UNSOLVED WHILE OTHERS HAVE A SURPRISING FINALE, AND MANY TURN OUT TO HAVE BEEN UNFORTUNATELY PREDICTABLE OR EASILY AVOIDED – REPRESENT AN INEXPLICABLE AND FASCINATING WAY OF LIFE, THAT OF ROCK 'N' ROLL. A WORLD WHERE ONE BURNS OUT INSTEAD OF FADING AWAY, AS KURT COBAIN WROTE IN HIS LAST LETTER, QUOTING NEIL YOUNG. AND – AS THE WHO SANG IN *MY GENERATION* – A WORLD WHERE IN ORDER TO BECOME A HERO IT IS BETTER TO DIE BEFORE GROWING OLD.

"I SEE MYSELF AS A HUGE
FIERY COMET,
A SHOOTING STAR.
EVERYONE STOPS,
POINTS UP AND GASPS
"OH LOOK AT THAT!"
THEN – WHOOSH, AND I'M GONE...
AND THEY'LL NEVER SEE
ANYTHING LIKE IT EVER AGAIN...
AND THEY WON'T BE ABLE
TO FORGET ME – EVER."

[Jim Morrison]

ROBERT JOHNSON

[8 May 1911
> 16 August 1938]

The Devil was lurking at a crossroad, which led to the birth of the blues. That was the legend of Robert Johnson, who supposedly made a pact with the Devil, exchanging his life for the gift of being able to play the guitar like no one else. The crossroad was in Clarksdale, Mississippi, where Highway 61 and Highway 49 intersect. It was Johnson himself who fuelled the myth about selling his soul by singing *Me and the Devil Blues* and *The Hellhound on My Trail*. But then, everything in his life was legendary.

Robert Johnson was probably born on 8 May 1911 at Hazlehurst, Mississippi to Julia Major Dodds and Noah Johnson. Julia was married to another man, Charles Dodds, who, because of a dispute with local landowners, had to leave Hazlehurst and change his name to Spencer. That is the first mystery. The child kept his stepfather's surname until 1929, when he signed his real name on the marriage certificate when he married 16 year-old Virginia Travis. When quite young he discovered the world of music and learned to play the harmonica and from then on his life was a continuous journey through the streets of a remote and mysterious America. Robert Johnson met his mentors – two other blues legends, Son House and Isaiah "Ike" Zimmerman – in Robinsonville and Hazlehurst, to which he had probably returned to look for his natural father. House and Zimmerman taught young Robert a little, but they both agreed that the boy was not very good at playing the guitar. At least not until that momentous meeting with

the Devil, which brought about a sudden musical miracle, when Johnson unexpectedly became the best guitarist around and began to travel in the Deep South.

From 1932, until his death, his life is virtually impossible to reconstruct. He played using at least eight different surnames, lived in the homes of his many women and played in all the blues joints in the region. His legacy consists of 29 songs, 16 of which he recorded in a single five-day session in November 1936. H.C. Speir, the owner of a record shop in Jackson, Mississippi and a talent scout, put him in contact with Ernie Oertle, who offered to record his music in Texas. A recording studio was set up in room 414 at the Gunther Hotel in San Antonio and Johnson left his mark on the story of the blues (it is said that he played facing the wall). Those sessions led to the release of a record, *Terraplane Blues*, which enjoyed fair success. Johnson had realised his dream of being not just another black person working in the cotton fields. A second recording session took place in 1937 in the Brunswick Records studio in Dallas, where he cut the remaining songs in his repertoire. He then began to travel, ranging from St. Louis to Memphis, Chicago, Detroit and the Mississippi Delta. Until one night in May 1938, when he paid his debt to the Devil at a club in Mississippi called Three Forks, which was also situated near an intersection (Highways 42 and 49) south of Memphis.

Johnson had a gig there with harmonica player Sonny Boy Williamson. Another musician,

Dave Honeyboy Edwards, was supposed to be with them but had not yet appeared. The club had become crowded. Many of the clients were women and one in particular kept staring at Johnson. He was known for being a ladies' man, which had gotten him into trouble in the past. The girl kept on staring and he reciprocated. Some people say the woman was the wife of the club owner, a ticklish situation. At a certain point, someone passed a bottle of whisky to the musicians. Sonny Boy threw it to the floor, warning Johnson never to drink from a bottle that someone offered and that had already been opened. Another bottle arrived and Johnson drank from it.

Since Honeyboy Edwards had not arrived, the two began to play. But Johnson was not feeling well. Sonny Boy couldn't believe that what he had feared had actually happened: the whisky had been poisoned; the jealous husband had taken his revenge. Johnson was taken to a home in Greenwood, a few miles away, and stayed in bed for a few days. He managed to get over the poisoning but then became ill with pneumonia. On 16 August 1938 he died at the age of 27. He was buried in an unmarked grave in a cemetery in Morgan City.

No one knows whether the Devil really exists or can teach the blues. What we do know is that the Robert Johnson legend had just begun:

"You may bury my body, ooh / down by the highway side / So my old evil spirit / can catch a Greyhound bus and ride." This is the the end of Johnson's song *Me and the Devil Blues.*

11 One of three existing photographs of Robert Johnson, taken in 1935. The legendary bluesman is seen with Johnny Shines, who accompanied him for years on his trips throughout the United States. "He was a very friendly person," Shines said of him, "but he was kind of a peculiar fellow."

BUDDY
HOLLY

The day the music died. The first great rock 'n' roll tragedy occurred on 3 February 1959 and was a rude awakening for America. Around 1.00 am a small plane crashed at Clear Lake, Iowa, near Mason City airport. It had been a freezing night and the plane had taken off only a few minutes earlier. The pilot, Roger Peterson, died in the crash, as did all the passengers – producer, and former DJ, J.P. Richardson, known as The Big Bopper, Mexican-Californian singer Ricardo Valenzuela, who better known as Ritchie Valens and the greatest American rock 'n' roll star, the Texan Charles Hardin Holley better known as Buddy Holly. A generation of pioneers of rock music was destroyed on that ill-fated night.

Buddy Holly was born on 7 September 1936 at Lubbock, Texas and began to play and sing at an early age, encouraged by his elder brothers Larry and Travis. In 1952 he formed the Buddy and Bob duo with his school friend Bob Montgomery and began to sing country and western songs in local talent shows, soon becoming a celebrity in the area. But recognition came about in 1955, when Elvis Presley went to Lubbock for the first time. On 15 October Buddy Holly opened Presley's show and discovered the rock 'n' roll sound. Fellow band member Sonny Curtis described this important moment: "From that day on we became rockabilly. [...] We turned into Elvis clones overnight."

Buddy Holly did not have Elvis Presley's sex appeal or stage presence, but he certainly knew how to write great songs. One of those was *That'll Be The Day*, his first 1957 success. It was the song that marked the definitive transformation of Buddy Holly: after an initial negative experience at Nashville with Decca Records, which insisted that he record only country songs, Buddy Holly worked in Norman Petty's recording studio in Clovis, New Mexico together with his drummer and friend Jerry Allison, where he created his unique sound, a sound that influenced the history of rock 'n' roll. On 1 March 1958 Buddy and his band, The Crickets, were touring the UK, where they conquered an entire generation of young British musicians. Paul McCartney was spellbound by their performance in the *Sunday Night at the London Palladium* television show and the Rolling Stones enjoyed their first success with a cover of the Crickets song *Not Fade Away*. The success story of the Crickets continued up to 1958 with seven singles making the Top 40 in America and then Buddy Holly married Maria Elena Santiago, a receptionist for Peer Southern Music, disbanded the Crickets and moved to Greenwich Village in New York City to concentrate on creating a new perspective for his music. But he had major financial problems and in order to solve them he accepted the General Artist Corporation's proposal of a three-week tour in the Midwest called Winter Dance Party. Buddy Holly assembled a new band, consisting of guitarist Tommy Allsup, drummer Carl Bunch and bass guitarist Waylon Jennings and set off on the tour on 27 January 1959. On the bill with Holly were Dion and the Belmonts, a vocal group from New York, the then unknown Frankie Sardo, Big Bopper and the new revelation of rock music, Ritchie Valens, who, at the age of 17 had just sold a million copies of his single *Donna / La Bamba*. From the outset the tour was beset with problems. The temperature in Minnesota, Wisconsin and Iowa was always below zero and the band's bus was in bad condition and had no heating at all. The Winter Dance Party became an increasingly more difficult adventure, with breakdowns, delays and musicians catching the flu. After the concert at Clear Lake, Buddy Holly was exhausted and decided to rent a small plane to get to the next stop of their tour in North Dakota. There was room for only three passengers on the plane. Tommy Allsup and Ritchie Valens flipped a coin and Allsup lost. Waylon Jennings gave his seat to Big Bopper, who had a fever. Buddy Holly joked with him: "You're going to get pneumonia on the bus." Waylon replied with a playful wisecrack that in hindsight is blood-curdling: "I hope your plane crashes." The day the music died: the first person who described the terrible day that marked the end of an epoch in the history of rock 'n' roll was Don McLean in his 1971 song *American Pie*. Buddy Holly rests in the cemetery of his hometown, Lubbock, Texas. But his music lives on.

13 Buddy Holly and his band, The Crickets, performing on the *Ed Sullivan Show* in December 1957, two years prior to the tragic plane crash that killed him as well as Ritchie Valens and Big Bopper. The date of Holly's death is considered in rock history as "the day the music died," a definition taken from the front page of a specially dedicated edition of the *Daily Mirror*.

"THE DAY THE MUSIC DIED"

[Daily Mirror]

EDDIE

COCHRAN

During the 1950s, rock 'n' roll music had been a call for rejuvenation, a rebellious style that had conquered a generation with its music, its look and its lifestyle, as well as through its personalities, who had become heroes. One of the latter was Eddie Cochran, a pioneer of rockabilly who influenced the future of rock 'n' roll. Cochran had been an elegantly dressed boy with a rebellious streak who could sing like Elvis but could also play the guitar, the piano, the bass guitar and the drums and who became a legend because he died when he was only 21, in a road accident during a UK tour.

Cochran had been born in Minnesota and had grown up in California. He made his debut in 1956 in the musical film *The Girl Can't Help It*, starring Jane Mansfield, in which he sang *Twenty Flight Rock*, which helped to make that movie one of the first celebrations of rock 'n' roll music and its lifestyle. November 1957 saw the release of his first and only album, *Singin' To My Baby*. The following year some of the most important songs in the history of rockabilly – such as *Summertime Blues* (which The Who covered in 1970) and *C'mon Everybody* – were produced. Eddie Cochran became part of the lost generation of rock together with his friends Buddy Holly and Ritchie Valens, both of whom died in a plane crash on 3 February 1959. Terribly upset by the accident (in which Big Bopper had also been killed), Eddie Cochran had wanted to give up making live music and concentrate instead on studio work but he had ended up accepting an invitation from London's Fosters agency to make a UK tour, with Gene Vincent, starting in Ipswich on 24 January 1960. The tour had ended on 16 April after a final week at the Hippodrome Club in Bristol. Eddie's fee, 1000 dollars a week, had been substantial but he had spent most of it on telephone calls. He had conquered

the British public but wanted to go back home, where his family were waiting for him, and where he had scheduled studio sessions with Snuffy Garret and also a probable appearance on the Ed Sullivan Show. On 16 April tour manager Patrick Tompkins knocked on his door at the Royal Hotel and gave him the flight ticket for the following day, when he was to leave at 1.00 pm from London Heathrow. Gene Vincent, however, was moving on to Paris, where he had other gigs scheduled. So the two, Cochran and Vincent, had decided to leave for London right after the final concert of the tour, together with Eddie's girlfriend, Sharon Sheeley. Tompkins found a taxi company with a night service and booked the journey. As the three were getting into the taxi, a Ford Consul, after the show Sharon noted some confetti inside it and the driver, George Martin, had explained that it had been used for a wedding earlier that afternoon.

There are many legends regarding that final journey of Eddie Cochran, who had been sitting in the back seat of the taxi with Sharon Sheeley and Gene Vincent. The driver had been inexperienced and might have been drunk; a marriage proposal had been whispered in the dead of night; the driver had taken the wrong road at Bath and had braked too quickly to double back. The only certainty is police officer R.S. McIntyre's report: "Fatal accident on Bath Road, Chippenham, at 11.50 pm on 16 April 1960." Sharon Sheeley, Gene Vincent and Patrick Tompkins had been injured and taken to St. Martin's Hospital in Bath. The driver was unhurt and was sentenced to six months in prison and fined 50 pounds for dangerous driving. Eddie Cochran's tombstone in the Forest Lawn Memorial Park at Cypress, California bears the inscription "If mere words can console us for the loss of our beloved Eddie, then our love for him was a false love."

15 The *Daily Mirror* front page with the news of the accidental death of Eddie Cochran, seen holding his guitar in pure rockabilly style. Critic Lester Bangs said the following about him: "Eddie may have imitated Elvis vocally even more than a dozen or so other stalwarts of the day such as Conway Twitty, but his influence on pop consciousness of the magnitude of The Beatles and The Who was deep and profound."

STU SUTCLIFFE

[23 June 1940 > 10 April 1962]

Stuart Sutcliffe was an artist, a boy of the 1950s thunderstruck by Buddy Holly and rock 'n' roll and had been a friend of John Lennon's during their time at Liverpool College of Art. Stu was one of several people sometimes called "The Fifth Beatle" and one of the great lost talents of rock music. He died of a brain haemorrhage at the age of 21 when the burgeoning Beatles had yet to set foot inside a recording studio. It had been Stu who had created the band's image yet he did not live to see it achieve greatness.

Stu Sutcliffe had been introduced to John Lennon by a mutual friend, Bill Harry, who, in 1961, founded and edited the "Mersey Beat" newspaper which launched the Liverpool sound in the UK. All three boys were students at Liverpool College of Art. Lennon had been one of the worst students while Sutcliffe had been one of the best. He shared an apartment at 3 Gambier Terrace with another promising artist in the college, illustrator Margaret Chapman. Stu and John immediately became good friends. They talked about art, literature, Buddy Holly and the new rock 'n' roll music that had been becoming popular in Liverpool. In 1960, John Lennon moved in with Sutcliffe. That was the beginning of the adventure of the most famous band in history.

Stu met Paul McCartney at the Casbah Coffee Shop (which belonged to the mother of the first Beatles drummer, Pete Best), who persuaded him to buy a bass guitar. Stu had studied piano and his father had taught him some guitar chords, but he was not an accomplished musician. However, he had just earned 65 pounds from the sale of one of his paintings at an exhibition and so could afford to buy a Hofner President 500/5 bass at Frank Hessey's Music Shop. The flat on Gambier Terrace soon became a rehearsal room for the band, which was initially called The Quarrymen and later The Beatals, The Silver Beetles, The Silver Beatles and, finally, The Beatles. According to legend, the idea for that name came during an evening spent at the Renshaw Hall bar in Liverpool: Stu, John and his girlfriend, Cynthia Powell, had been trying to think of a name similar to that of Buddy Holly's band, The Crickets, and they came up with The Beatals. At the beginning of 1960, the band went on a tour of Scotland, opening for Johnny Gentle, and in August of that year, after Pete Best had become their drummer, they made their first trip to Hamburg. Their agent, Allan Williams (the owner of one of the first clubs the Beatles played in, the Jacaranda in Liverpool), had decided to have them go to Germany after having seen the success enjoyed there by another of his bands, Derry and the Seniors. So John Lennon, Paul McCartney, George Harrison, Pete Best and Stu Sutcliffe departed for Hamburg on 17 August 1960 with a contract for 15 pounds a week and an engagement at the Indra Club and the Kaiserkeller, two clubs in the St. Pauli red light district.

The trip to Hamburg is a rock 'n' roll legend: the band members had lived in a horrible room behind the screen of a movie theatre, the Bambi Kino; George Harrison had been deported because he had been under age; John Lennon had provoked members of the audience, calling them krauts and telling them that England had won the war, thus triggering applause on the part of the British sailors present; Paul McCartney and Pete Best had also been arrested and deported for arson because they had set fire to a tapestry.

But the gigs in Hamburg helped the Beatles to play better and to learn stage presence, which were to become the bases of their greatness and also created their image. Sutcliffe was not a very proficient bass player and often played with his back to the audience; and he sang only one song, the cover they performed of Elvis Presley's *Love Me Tender*. But he became the first band member to appear on stage with tight jeans and wearing a pair of dark sunglasses. And he was also the first to meet a local girl, Astrid Kirchherr. That occurred in the Kaiserkeller. Astrid had been a photographer and went to see the new band that had just arrived from England. The next day she invited the Beatles to her mother's house, in the upper class district of Altona, and showed them her bedroom, which was painted entirely in black, with silver foil decoration and a huge tree branch hanging from the ceiling. Stu immediately fell in love with this sophisticated and fascinating girl and they began a relationship. Astrid set about helping to create the Beatles' style, supposedly suggesting that the band adopt a hairstyle that was very popular in Germany at the time, the moptop. As Astrid herself declared, the first band member to stop using Brylcreem on his hair, as had been the typical rockabilly fashion, and to have her cut his hair was Sutcliffe. He also dressed in her clothes: leather trousers, jackets without a collar, and blouses. Thus was born the Beatles' look. Their love story was a beautiful fairy tale, a meeting of two artists. Stu decided to leave the Beatles in July 1961 and to return to his art studies. He left his bass guitar to Paul McCartney but asked him not to change the strings even though Paul was left-handed, that is, for him the strings were "upside-down." Stu was not accepted for the Art Teachers Diploma course at Liverpool Art College, so, instead, he enrolled at Hamburg College of Art, where he studied with the famous pop artist Eduardo Paolozzi. His life with Astrid and his artistic career had just begun.

But, in 1962, he collapsed during an art class. For some time he had been suffering from migraine and had been acutely sensitive to light. Astrid's mother had several physicians visit him, and they had suggested he return to England to be treated. But another collapse proved fatal: on 10 April 1962 Stu had been feeling unwell and collapsed again. Astrid called an ambulance, but he was pronounced dead upon arrival at hospital. He was only 21. Who knows what might have happened had he continued as the fifth Beatle.

17 Stuart Sutcliffe and John Lennon playing on stage at the Top Ten Club in Hamburg in 1961, during the Beatles' first tour of Germany. The two became friends at Liverpool College of Art. According to John Lennon, Sutcliffe was "the star of the school, a true artist."

SAM COOKE

[22 January 1931
> 11 December 1964]

Sam Cooke liked women very much. His wife Barbara was well aware of that but for a long time had accepted his extramarital affairs. He was the King of Soul, with no less than 29 hits in the US Top40 between 1957 and 1964. He was the idol of the African-American community and very active in the civil rights movement. Their marriage was already floundering, especially after the tragic death of their 18-month old son Vincent, who drowned in the Cooke's swimming pool in 1963. Sam had been out of town and had accused his wife Barbara of not having kept a close watch on their son. From that time on he did nothing but accept out-of-town gigs whenever he could, thus giving vent to the desperation in his music, as well as in the women who were attracted by his fame and velvety voice.

Sam Cooke began singing with his brothers in a gospel group called The Singing Children. In 1950 he became leader of the Soul Stirrers, which recorded with Specialty Records of Chicago and became one of the most important gospel bands in the United States. Then he decided to take black music to the pop charts and, in 1956, tried his luck with the single *Lovable*, which he released under the pseudonym Dale Cook. His voice was unmistakable and his distinctive manner of merging gospel and secular music laid the foundation for soul. *Lovable* sold 25,000 copies and launched his career. He left The Soul Stirrers and signed a contract with Keen Records. He devoted himself to the new soul genre with the same tireless energy that had led to his success in gospel music and in 1957 his single *You Send Me* was number one on two Billboard charts. Subsequently, his career took off thanks to other singles such as *Wonderful World*, *Chain Gang* (number two in the 1960 charts), *Cupid* and *Twistin' the Night Away*. Sam Cooke became the King of Soul. At that time he also began to take an active part in the civil rights movement after hearing Bob Dylan's *Blowin' in the Wind*. He was both amazed and moved that such a forceful song,

addressing racism and injustice, could have been written by a white person. On 8 October 1963, while at Shreveport, Louisiana during a tour, he and his band members stopped in a motel reserved for whites only. He asked for a room and was met by a refusal. The motel manager phoned the police and the King of Soul was arrested. That regrettable incident was the inspiration for what was to become Sam Cooke's most famous song, *A Change Is Gonna Come*. It is said that he wrote the first draft of this song while on a tour bus after having witnessed a sit-in demonstration in Durham, North Carolina: "It's been a long time coming, but I know a change is gonna come." Martin Luther King was very fond of the song, which became a kind of anthem for the civil rights movement. It was released on 1 March 1964, on the album *Ain't That Good News*. That same year his album *Sam Cooke Live at the Copa* was number one in the charts. Everything was going well.

In just a few years the boy from Clarksdale, Mississippi who had grown up in the gospel churches of Chicago, had become a star. Women went crazy over him and he reciprocated. Until one last rave night that ended in the worst possible way and with a finale wrapped in controversy. On 11 December 1964, Sam Cooke went to Martoni's, an Italian restaurant in Hollywood, to attend a party in his honour with many of his friends and collaborators. His wife Barbara stayed at home, something that had become somewhat of a habit. Sam Cooke drank a lot. He spotted a very attractive girl at one of the tables, 22 year-old Elisa Boyer. He invited her to another club and she accepted. They left Martoni's in Cooke's automobile and went to a place he was very familiar with, the Hacienda Motel at 9137 Figueroa Street, Long Beach, where he had been many times before. It was a very discrete establishment where no questions were asked. Sam and Elisa registered as Mr. and Mrs. Smith at 2.30 am. At the reception desk was a lady named Bertha Franklin.

19 "I was born by the river in a little tent/Oh and just like the river I've been running ever since/It's been a long, a long time coming/But I know a change gonna come, oh yes it will." *A Change Is Gonna Come* by Sam Cooke, seen here during a recording session in 1959, became an anthem for the Civil Rights Movement in America.

20 From 1957 to 1964 Sam Cooke was the King of Soul, with 29 hits in the American Top 40. Unfortunately, his brilliant career was cut short the evening he was murdered in a motel, as reported by this *New York Times* headline.

20-21 Sam Cooke had a ringside seat when Muhammad Ali (then Cassius Clay) defeated Sonny Liston and became the heavyweight champion of the world on 25 February 1964. The two sang *The Gang's All Here* together on the Harry Carpenter show broadcast by the BBC.

"SAM COOKE SLAIN IN COAST MOTEL"

[The New York Times]

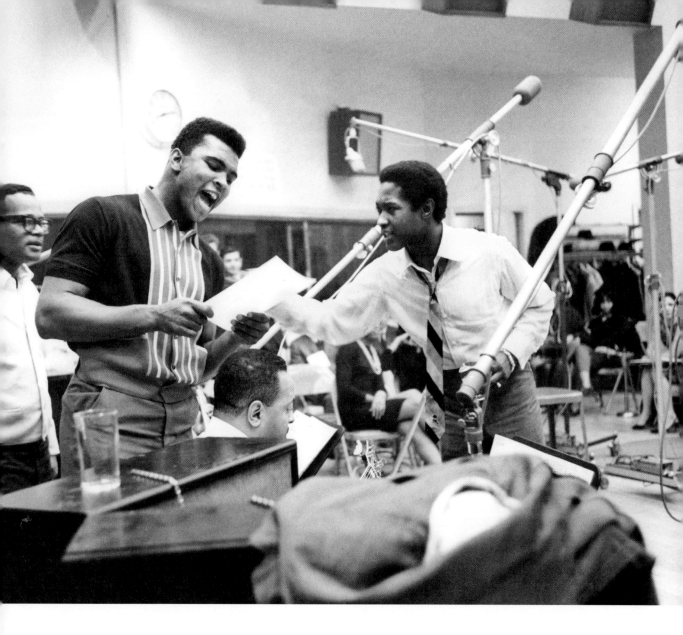

It looked like yet another "night of sin" so typical of stars but something went wrong. To this day, no one knows exactly what occurred in that motel room. At a certain point Sam Cooke rushed out of the room in a fury and ran to the reception desk. He was half-naked, wearing only a jacket and a pair of shoes, and was obviously in a drunken state. He shouted that the girl had disappeared after stealing his clothes and wallet. He was convinced that she was hiding somewhere in the motel office. Bertha Franklin told him she knew nothing about it; he did not believe her and grabbed her. Franklin broke loose and found her pistol. There was a shot and Sam Cooke fell to the floor: "Lady, you shot me." Soon afterwards, Elisa Boyer called the police from a phone booth and said she had been kidnapped. Another call arrived at the police station from Evelyn Carr, the owner of the Hacienda Motel. Bertha Franklin was acquitted for legitimate self-defence. Elisa Boyer stated that Sam Cooke had tried to rape her and that she had run away, taking his clothes with her by mistake. The singer's wallet, which had been full of money, was never found. No one could believe that the King of Soul could have died in that way. But the Los Angeles police closed the case. Elisa Boyer was arrested for prostitution a short time later.

BOBBY FULLER

[22 October 1942 > 18 July 1966]

23 Bobby Fuller with his band, the Bobby Fuller Four, in 1960. His death on 18 July 1966 is one of rock's great mysteries. Although it was officially registered as a suicide by Los Angeles police, it was rumoured that it was a Mafia murder to pocket a million dollar life insurance payout.

Bobby Fuller's death remains one of rock music's great unsolved mysteries. A death full of questions without answers that ended the promising career of one of the pioneers of rock 'n' roll. Fuller was the author of a song that, in time, became an anthem, *I Fought the Law*, a rebellious cry against the system that later fascinated punk musicians and bands, from the Clash to Green Day, and which sounded even more ironic after his demise. Bobby Fuller was a Texan, like Buddy Holly, and was overwhelmed by rock 'n' roll at the age of 12, after seeing Elvis Presley on television. He learned to play the piano, drums and trumpet while his brother Randy began playing the guitar. Randy was sent to a military college and, when he returned, he found out that Bobby, in the meantime, had also learned to play the guitar and had written his first songs, including *You're in Love* and *Guess We Fall in Love*, which were released by Yucca Records in November 1961.

Thanks to the success of his debut, which sold 3,000 copies, Bobby began to play bars and clubs in El Paso. In his back yard he built a small home studio, with two microphones and a second-hand mixing board he had borrowed from a local radio station, and created his own label, which he called Exeter Records. Bobby was totally dedicated to music and did everything on his own, aiming at become a star like his idols. The great occasion happened in 1964 after he went to California in an Oldsmobile that his mother Loraine drove: Bobby and his band (called the Bobby Fuller Four) were signed up by the Del-Fi label of producer Bob Keane, the same

person who had discovered and launched Ritchie Valens. Within two years Bobby had succeeded in making his way on the Los Angeles rock 'n' roll scene thanks to his cover of *I Fought the Law* by The Crickets, which he had recorded for the first time in his El Paso 'studio'. It was released in 1965 and, thanks to the support of the LA rock radio, it earned ninth place in the hit parade chart. Thus, the stage was set for the Texas boy to become a star. Bobby also recorded one of the last songs written by his idol Buddy Holly, *Love's Made a Fool of You* and in 1966 the Bobby Fuller Four went on a tour of the United States, while their first official album, *I Fought the Law*, went on sale.

In the meantime Los Angeles was becoming psychedelic and hip and Bobby Fuller, wanting to experiment with the new scene, was determined to organize a new band. On 17 July 1966 he told Bob Keane that he had made an appointment with some musicians for the following day in the Del-Fi offices. He had also intended to see his guitarist Jim Reese, who wanted to sell him his automobile, a Jaguar XKE. He did not go to either appointment. And here the mystery begins. At 5.00 pm on 18 July the musicians went to Fuller's house to see if he was there – in vain. His mother spotted his Oldsmobile, the one he had used for the trip from El Paso to California, parked outside his apartment. She opened the door and found Bobby in the driver's seat with his hands on the key, which was in the ignition. He was dead, his body soaked in gasoline. He had large bruises on his chest and face, and one finger of his right hand was

broken. On the seat next to him was a half-empty can of gasoline. The Los Angeles County coroner established that Bobby had died three hours earlier from asphyxiation after having inhaled gasoline fumes. His mother stated that at 1.00 am that night Bobby had received a phone call and had gone out. The last person to see him alive was his landlord, Lloyd Esinger, with whom Fuller had drunk a couple of beers at 3.00 am. "He was in a really good mood," Esinger had said. The police closed the case after a very hasty investigation, during which they did not even take fingerprints from the gasoline can, and their absurd report attributed his death to suicide. Bobby Fuller was buried in the Forest Lawn Cemetery, Burbank, but his demise triggered a series of serious questions. How was it possible that a 24-year old man with a brilliant career in rock 'n' roll ahead of him and such passion for music, decided to commit suicide? Bobby had a life insurance policy for one million dollars. The beneficiaries were the Del-Fi investors, among whom, it was said, were important members of the Los Angeles Mob. The police refused to undertake any further investigation and closed the case. Four days after Bobby's funeral, three armed men showed up at the apartment of Jim Reese and Dalton Powell, the Bobby Fuller Four drummer. The next morning the two got into their car and returned to El Paso: "Maybe for some people we were an investment and were worth more dead than alive," Jim Reese stated years later. In fact, Del-Fi had made a huge amount of money nine years earlier, after Ritchie Valens had died.

OTIS REDDING

In August 1967 Otis Redding was on tour in the United States with the Bar-Kays. One day, while on the houseboat of his friend Earl "Speedo" Sims, moored in Sausalito, California, he wrote the first line of a new song. He also gave it a temporary title, *The Dock of the Bay*. Otis Redding had just left his mark with a memorable performance at the Monterey Pop Festival, where he had been the closing act of the second evening and had been accompanied by Booker T & the M.G.'s (they had been preceded by Jefferson Airplane). That was the first time that Otis Redding had performed for such a large white audience. Earlier, in 1966, he had given a series of concerts at the Whisky a Go Go in Los Angeles.

Otis Redding had been the most important performer for Stax Records in Memphis, for which he released his first album, 1964's *Pain in My Heart*, and was already becoming a soul music legend. His *Try a Little Tenderness* reached number 25 on Billboard's Hot 100 chart. *Respect* became an anthem for the African-American community and the concerts he played in Europe helped him to conquer a wider public. In 1967, Otis heard the Beatles' *Sgt. Pepper's Lonely Hearts Club Band* and decided to change his style. He wanted to continue to conquer the white audiences and experimented with new melodies that were not so connected to the roots of soul and rhythm and blues, as the music recorded for Stax. Thus, during the tour promoting the *King & Queen* album, Otis continued to add verses to his new song, *(Sittin' On) The Dock of the Bay*, writing them down wherever he happened to be and on whatever was to hand at the time – restaurant napkins and hotel note pads for example. On 22 November 1967 he went to the Stax studios in Memphis, with his guitarist Steve Cropper, and recorded the song. He returned on 8 December to finish it but had not yet finished writing the lyrics so, during the fade out at the end of the recording session, Redding whistled to mark the point so that when he returned to it he could pick up the song at that point for the final verse. He never did return to it and the whistling in *(Sittin' On) The Dock of the Bay* became a part of music folklore. A few days later, Redding and the Bar-Kays left on his private plane (a Beechcraft H18) for a series of concerts. On 9 December 1967 they had been in Cleveland, where they had participated in the *Upbeat* TV show and had played three gigs at a small club called Leo's Casino.

The following day he had had a date at the University of Wisconsin, Madison. Weather conditions had been very poor; torrential rain and dense fog and, although advised against it, Redding decided to fly so as not to miss the concert. Aboard the Beechcraft were Otis, his personal assistant Matthew Kelley, and five members of the Bar-Kays. Two other members, Carl Sims and James Alexander, made the trip with a commercial airline because the Beechcraft had been full. At 3.30 pm, the pilot, Richard Fraser, had asked for permission to land at Truax Field in Madison. But something had gone wrong. The Beechcraft descended rapidly and crashed into Lake Monona. The impact had been terrific, ending the career of one of the most brilliant stars of black music and that of his extraordinary band. The only survivor of the accident was one of the Bar-Kays, Ben Cauley. The last thing he remembered was having unfastened his seat belt while the plane was spiralling downwards. He then came to in the ice-cold water of Lake Monona, clutching a seat cushion. Otis Redding's body was found the following day. The symbol of soul music, the voice that had taken the history of African-American music almost everywhere, now rests in the ranch that he had had built in his home town, Macon, Georgia. And *(Sittin' On) The Dock of the Bay* remains forever unfinished.

25 Otis Redding in Paris in 1962. His European concerts and his participation in the Monterey Pop Festival unleashed the famous traditional soul sound of Stax Records on the rock public.

26 Otis Redding was born in Macon, Georgia in 1941. He left school when he was 15 to support his family by working in Little Richard's backing band, The Upsetters. In 1964 he released his album *Pain in My Heart*.

27 12 December 1967: the wreck of the Beechcraft H18 used by Otis Redding and his band, the Bar-Kays, is salvaged from Lake Monona, near Madison, Wisconsin. The *Wisconsin State Journal* had the unhappy task of informing the music world of the terrible airplane crash.

"SINGER OTIS REDDING, BAND
DIE IN LAKE MONONA CRASH"

[Wisconsin State Journal]

BRIAN
JONES

[28 February 1942 > 3 July 1969]

One of the great mysteries in the history of rock music was Brian Jones's drowning in the swimming pool of his villa at Cotchford Farm. He was only 27. Brian Jones was one of the founders of the greatest rock band in the world, the Rolling Stones, but in the last years of his life he became more and more estranged from the band. His life was intense and controversial, his talent eclectic. Furthermore, Brian Jones was a rebel well before the transgressive lifestyle of the Rolling Stones had conquered the world. By 1961 he already had three children by three different women. His IQ was above average but he left school when he was 17 and travelled throughout Northern Europe and Scandinavia, surviving by busking with his guitar.

A crucial meeting in the history of rock took place in London in the early 1960s, in the Ealing Jazz Club: Brian Jones was playing a song by Elmore James, *Dust My Broom*, with Alexis Korner's band. Mick Jagger and Keith Richards were also in the club. On 2 May 1962, Brian Jones placed an advertisement in the magazine *Jazz News*, asking musicians to audition for rhythm and blues sessions at the Bricklayer's Arms pub. The first person to respond was pianist Ian Stewart, while guitarist Dick Taylor, drummer Tony Chapman, and Mick Jagger and Keith Richards followed soon after. The sessions at the Bricklayer's Arms led to the birth of the Rolling Stones. The line-up was complete in 1963 with the arrival of bass guitarist Bill Wyman and drummer Charlie Watts. And it was Brian Jones who chose the name of the new band. He was trying to

arrange a gig with the owner of a club, who asked him what the band was called. There was a moment of silence and then Brian saw a Muddy Waters album on the floor, the first track of which was *Rollin' Stone*, so he replied: "The Rolling Stones."

In the early years Brian Jones worked hard promoting the band and considered himself to be its leader. The arrival of Andrew Loog Oldham, who became the Stones' manager in 1963, changed the configuration of the band. Oldham urged the Stones to write original material (as the Beatles did) and not only play cover versions of blues, and based the Stones' image on Mick Jagger's charisma. Brian felt his role in the band was diminishing. He wanted the Rolling Stones to remain a blues band, after all it was his band, and he seemed to lose interest in it. And yet his rhythmic guitar was the basis of the sound that had launched them, as was his harmonica (he had taught Jagger to play this instrument). However, when the band was at the height of its creative explosion, in 1966 and 1967, Brian seemed regenerated and became the pure artist of the band, lending new colours and sounds to the songs. His talent and his ability to play a great many instruments led the band to experiment: he used a sitar on *Paint it Black*, a recorder on *Ruby Tuesday*, a dulcimer on *Lady Jane* and psychedelia on *Their Satanic Majesties Request* (1967).

The problem was that constant and increasing use of drugs and alcohol jeopardised Brian's physical and mental health. As his fellow band members stated, there were two

Brian Jones. One was creative and sensitive, the other was arrogant and presumptuous. He was respected by other musicians of the time. The Beatles invited him to play sax on *You Know My Name*, and he introduced Jimi Hendrix to the audience at the Monterey Pop Festival. But he was not getting along with his fellow band members, partly because he was often in no condition to play. To top things off, in 1967 his girlfriend Anita Pallenberg left him for Keith Richards. Again, the police began to target the band for its nonconformist lifestyle, and Jones was arrested twice for drug possession, in 1967 and in 1968. The episode estranged him even more. Brian took part in the recordings of *Beggars Banquet* (1968), as usual playing several different instruments and singing in the choruses of *Sympathy for the Devil*. But, from that time on he did very little with the Rolling Stones. In *Let it Bleed* (1969) he played on only two songs, *You Got the Silver* and *Midnight Rambler*. Jagger and Richards decided the band had to go on tour to the United States, where they had not played for three years, but Brian could not get a visa because of his drug possession convictions. The breakup occurred on 8 June 1969, when the Rolling Stones told Jones that the band he had founded would continue without him. He was replaced by Mick Taylor.

Richards later recalled that Brian's main problem was not music. It was that even if things were going well he was somehow compelled to ruin everything. Richards admitted he had a demon inside, but only one, while Brian

probably had 45 more. It was a question of pride, which ate into him. Brian retired to his villa at Cotchford Farm with his Swedish girlfriend Anna Wohlin. He was planning to form a new band and contacted his friends Alexis Korner, Ian Stewart and Mitch Mitchell. He wanted to write, work on producing, and shoot a film. But his life ended mysteriously on the evening of 9 July 1969.

In the world of the Rolling Stones, fame, wealth and the myth of transgression attracted people of every kind. Among these was Tom Keylock, who had become the band's security expert. When Jagger told him he was looking for someone to build a wall around his Stargroves house, Tom called an old school friend, Frank Thorogood. After Stargroves, Frank also rebuilt Redlands, Keith Richards's villa. He immediately showed himself to be rather unreliable. He was not used to rock stars and their wealth, and soon took advantage of his position. To begin with, he stole several items from Richards's home, including one of his guitars. Keylock, who was becoming more and more influential in the Stones clan, persuaded Brian Jones to entrust Thorogood with various handyman jobs at Cotchford Farm. Frank moved into Brian's house, with his girlfriend Janet Lawson and some friends, and they spent more time drinking than working. One day, a beam in the kitchen ceiling fell and almost hit Anna Wohlin. Brian Jones had had enough, but he couldn't manage to fire Frank. He finally decided to deal with the problem on the evening of 2 July 1969. He invited Frank and Janet for a drink to clarify matters.

What actually occurred after that is still a mystery. According to some testimony, there was a kind of party at Cotchford, also attended by some of Frank's labourers. Others claim that only Brian, Anna, Frank and Janet were there that evening. What is certain is that Brian decided to take a swim. Anna went back into the house to answer the phone and when she returned Brian was dead. He had drowned in the pool. He had been an excellent swimmer and the examining physicians found no significant traces of alcohol or drugs in his system: an inexplicable death that soon became an unsolved mystery.

30-31 Brian Jones and the Rolling Stones during the shooting of *The Rolling Stones Rock and Roll Circus*, 11 December 1968. The Who, Jethro Tull, Taj Mahal, Marianne Faithfull, John Lennon, Yoko Ono and Eric Clapton also took part in the show.

The media even conjectured up a plot on the part of Keith Richards and Mick Jagger, neither of whom attended Brian's funeral service. The Rolling Stones dedicated a free concert to Brian, held in Hyde Park on 5 July 1969, which opened with one of his favourite songs, *I'm Yours and I'm Hers* by Johnny Winter. The mystery continued until 1994, when Frank Thorogood, on his deathbed, confessed to Tom

Keylock that something terrible had occurred in the swimming pool that evening. His account goes as follows.

He and his friends could not put up with Brian any longer. They teased him, wanting to see if he really was such a good swimmer and held his head under water. The horseplay ended tragically. But there is no reliable evidence regarding Thorogood's confession, nor were any

witnesses found. In 2009, the police re-opened the case, but closed it again for lack of evidence.

Brian Jones lies at rest in a bronze coffin in Cheltenham cemetery. Charlie Watts said of him: "Brian didn't live long enough to do everything he had spoken or thought of doing. I don't know whether he would have realised anything. In any case, he had no chance to."

32 and 33 An engrossed Brian Jones in two close-ups taken in 1966. The versatile musician taught himself to play the sitar, drawing inspiration from George Harrison who once said that there was nothing in Brian's problems that a bit more love would not have solved and that he had never been understood.

Evening News

RANGOL CSID design award 1969 reflex

London Thursday July 3, 1969. No. 27,204 5d.

Night Special

21st birthday? Give an AVIA watch

Swim pool clue of 'the puffer'

ANNA, BLONDE IN A BLACK BIKINI, GIVES KISS-OF-LIFE

HERE BRIAN JONES DIED, ON A HOT DARK NIGHT

By HARRY JONES
BRIAN JONES, 25-year-old ex-guitarist of the Rolling Stones, died suddenly today during a midnight swim.

He had been swimming in the pool at his 15th century Sussex farmhouse at Hartfield, tucked away in a fold of the rolling Ashdown Forest.

Modernising

Russian envoy in Brooke talks

By MAURICE ROMILLY

Chaos again on Tubes

HARASSED London Transport organisers were keeping their fingers crossed for tonight's mass City exodus as they struggled to cope with the effects of the strike of 250 signalmen on the Underground.

DILEMMA FOR NUR CHIEFS
By R. J. FINNEMORE

Closing Prices

JIMI HENDRIX

In his hands the electric guitar caught fire. Jimi Hendrix was sheer energy, a thunderbolt creating a psychedelic and wild world in which blues, rock and soul combined to create totally new music. No other guitarist had such a strong impact on the evolution of the instrument. All the great guitarists of the 1960s, including Jeff Beck, Eric Clapton, Pete Townshend and Les Paul, bowed with respect before his talent. When he wore his Fender Stratocaster, Jimi Hendrix became a god of rock, a psychedelic shaman, a gypsy king of a new world, a genius destined to burn himself out quickly, consumed by his very creativity.

Born in Seattle to a poor family, Hendrix was a young black man without a future who enlisted in the army in order not to end up in prison. His career began with his fellow soldier Billy Cox in the Chitlin' Circuit of blues clubs for African Americans in the Southern United States, where he lived like a vagabond. He already played the guitar extremely well, like no one else. With his natural talent, continuous practice and maniacal perfectionism he totally mastered the blues. But there was something else, a mysterious power. It was as if his music arrived from another planet. In 1964 he joined The Royal Company, Little Richard's band, who had him play in the background together with all the other musicians. The same thing occurred with the Isley Brothers and King Curtis. He did bizarre things, played harsh and loud notes and generally behaved in an eccentric manner. His genius had not yet been discovered. In 1965 he went to New York, in search of fame and fortune, and while he was playing at the Cheetah Club on 53rd Avenue he was noticed by Chas Chandler, bass guitarist with The Animals, who had become a talent scout and manager and who was extremely impressed by Hendrix's ability. It was Linda Keith, Keith Richards' girlfriend, who had told Chandler to go listen to this unknown phenomenon play. After the gig, Chas went to see Hendrix in his dressing room and asked him if he would go with him to London.

Jimi arrived at London's Heathrow Airport in September 1966. When the police saw him arriving, dressed like a psychedelic shaman, they stopped him and questioned him for hours. No one had ever seen anyone looking like that, but in the free and sparkling atmosphere of swinging London in 1966, Jimi Hendrix's talent was finally recognised. Within a year he had met all the leading musicians of the time, including the Beatles, the Rolling Stones, Eric Clapton and Pete Townshend, who greatly appreciated his musicianship and helped him to express it. Jimi formed the Jimi Hendrix Experience with Mitch Mitchell and Noel Redding and his debut album, *Are You Experienced* (1967), went to number two in the British charts, just behind the Beatles' Sgt. *Pepper's Lonely Hearts Club Band*. Yet, when he returned to America he was still relatively unknown. Paul McCartney and Brian Jones persuaded the organisers to let him play at the Monterey Pop Festival on 18 June 1967 in the first great Summer of Love event. Jimi began his performance with a cover of Bob Dylan's *Like a Rolling Stone* and ended it by burning and smashing his guitar to the notes of *Wild Thing*. The guitar burned and the rock world had found a new god, whose career was brief but brilliant. That same year saw the release of his second album, *Axis: Bold As Love*, which went to number three in the American charts. In 1968 Hendrix went to the Record Plant in New York and Olympic Studios in London and began work on a monumental double album with some of the best musicians of the time: Dave Mason, Chris Wood and Steve Winwood of Traffic, drummer Buddy Miles, Jack Casady of Jefferson Airplane and keyboardist Al Kooper. The album was *Electric Ladyland*. Jimi's overwhelming creativity and talent would never again be more concentrated than on that album. During the subsequent two years, the last of his life, Jimi tried to form a new band, the Band of Gypsys, with drummer Buddy Miles and bassist Billy Cox, and to record another album, *First Rays of the New Rising Sun*. But *Electric Ladyland* already contained the best of his art. The high point of his career was as the closing act at Woodstock on 18 August 1969 and his psychedelic interpretation of the American national anthem, which was considered the manifesto of the anti-Vietnam War protest and of a generation that wanted to change the world. That upward striving towards something special, absolute and amazing that did not yet exist, was what made Jimi Hendrix the greatest and was,

37 Jimi Hendrix, the "psychedelic shaman," immortalised in a 1968 photograph. Hendrix once declared: "When the power of love overcomes the love of power the world will know peace."

38 and 39 The Jimi Hendrix Experience: Mitch Mitchell, Jimi Hendrix and Noel Redding. The band's first official concert took place on 13 October 1966 in Evreux, France. Hendrix released three albums with this band: *Are You Experienced*, *Axis: Bold As Love* and *Electric Ladyland*.

perhaps, the reason why his life was so brief, consumed as it was by talent that was too powerful and by an unbridled vision of life. Jimi Hendrix burned together with his guitar. In one of his last photographs he is seen embracing a black Stratocaster guitar.

Death arrived in the city that had launched him, London. Jimi was with one of his many girlfriends, Monika Danneman. They lived in a flat in the Samarkand Hotel, at 22 Lansdowne Crescent, Notting Hill. He spent his last day as a star, first posing for a photography service, then doing some shopping at Kensington Market and attending a reception at the home of Lord Philip Harvey's son, whom he had met casually on the street. He drank wine and smoked some hashish. At 11.00 pm there was another party at the home of a friend, Peter Cameron, where he consumed some amphetamine. Then Jimi went to Monika's flat. He was exhausted and wanted to sleep, so he took a packet of Monika's sleeping pills, Vesparax, a very strong brand that no longer exists. He took nine pills, a quantity well above a prescribed dose. At 7.00 am the following morning the two breakfasted and then went back to sleep. Monika woke up at 10.20 am and went out to buy some cigarettes. She claimed that Jimi was sleeping peacefully at the time. When she returned she found him unconscious, lying in his own vomit. She tried to telephone his personal physician but in her panicky state couldn't find the number. She then phoned Eric Burdon of War, with whom Hendrix had played his last concert two days earlier, at Ronnie Scott's club in Soho, and he told her to call an ambulance immediately. The ambulance arrived at 11.27 am but Jimi Hendrix was already dead. The combination of amphetamine, alcohol and sleeping pills had been lethal. His body was taken to Seattle, at his family's request, and was buried in the Greenwood Memorial Park in Renton. On his tomb is a sculpture of a Fender Stratocaster guitar.

"THE STORY OF LOVE… IS HELLO AND GOODBYE… UNTIL WE MEET AGAIN"

[Daily Mirror]

40-41 5 October 1968: Jimi Hendrix performing at the International Center in Honolulu. On the occasion of his death the *Daily Mirror* paid tribute to the great guitarist by quoting what he said about love — made up of "hellos" and "goodbyes," until the next "hello."

JANIS JOPLIN

[19 January 1943 > 4 October 1970]

Janis Joplin was the best female expression of the blues spirit. She was also the greatest white singer in the 1960s and one of the most important rock stars of all time, a symbol, together with Jimi Hendrix and Jim Morrison, of an incredible period of artistry and madness. And like Jimi Hendrix and Jim Morrison, Janis Joplin died in the early 1970s when only 27, overwhelmed by a fervent but self-destructive creativity. She was called Pearl because she was small, precious and fragile.

Janis was born in Port Arthur, Texas to a typical American middle class family. She had two siblings, Michael and Laura, but grew up with a group of friends who, like her, were outcasts or mavericks and who had rejected the rules of Texan society and discovered the blues through the records of Bessie Smith and Lead Belly. "At school I was a misfit. I read, I painted, I didn't hate niggers," she said. From the outset Janis personified the rebellion of a generation that caused an upheaval in 1960s society. She attended the University of Texas at Austin but didn't complete her studies. The campus newspaper published an article about her that began as follows: "She goes barefooted when she feels like it, wears Levi's to class because they're more comfortable, and carries her Autoharp with her everywhere she goes so that in case she gets the urge to break into song it will be handy. Her name is Janis Joplin." Major influences in her life were the great blues singers and the Beat generation poets.

In 1963 Janis went to San Francisco and settled in Haight-Ashbury, a rather run-down neighbourhood inhabited by many African-Americans and bohemians that would become the "birthplace" of the hippy counterculture. For Janis that was a period of excess, marked by drug abuse, bottles of Southern Comfort and unsuccessful love affairs, all of which triggered the inner torment that she expressed in her music. But that was also the period of her first songs, a session of seven blues standards, that she recorded with Jorma Kaukonen, the future guitarist of Jefferson Airplane. However, Janis was already a self-destructive person before becoming a rock star. Besides Southern Comfort she consumed huge quantities of amphetamine, and also tried heroin. At that stage her friends persuaded her to return to Port Arthur in 1965 and even paid her bus fare. For a year she seemed to live what could be considered a normal existence. She enrolled at Lamar University in Beaumont, Texas, she shook off the drug and alcohol habits and she even became engaged to a man who then abandoned her, bringing about yet another period of heartache.

Music became her life once again. She moved to Austin, where she played in blues clubs and was noticed by promoter Chet Helms, who persuaded her to go back to San Francisco to team up with a psychedelic rock band he was managing, Big Brother and the Holding Company. That was the beginning of a triumphant and brief career during which Janis became the rock legend Pearl. Her first major performance was at the Avalon Ballroom in San Francisco on 10 June 1966 and the following year the band released their debut album, *Big Brother and the Holding Company* and on 18 June 1967 played at the Monterey Pop Festival, the first major rock and Summer of Love event. Like Jimi Hendrix, Janis Joplin went onstage as a virtual unknown and when she left the stage, after a sensational interpretation of Big Mama Thornton's *Ball and Chain,* she had become an established star. A star that began to blaze once again with alcohol and drug abuse during the period she spent with the band in a hippy community in Lagunitas, California. The demons took hold of her soul again and consigned it to the cursed blues legend. On 12 August 1968 Big Brother and the Holding Company released their second album, *Cheap Thrills,* and it went to number one in the charts. The fourth track of the album was a cover of a rhythm & blues success by Aretha Franklin's sister Erma Franklin, *Piece of My Heart.* Joplin's rendition radically changed the original, filling it with pain, love and desperation. When *Piece of My Heart* came out an entire generation that had dreamed to the rhythm of rock fell in love with the

---

42 and 43 "Wild Girl of Pop Dies." *Daily Mirror* headline, 6 October 1970. A tribute to the rebellious, nonconformist spirit of Janis Lyn Joplin, which is also evident in the photo on the following page.

fragile and restless woman who became a fury on stage with a voice that went straight to one's heart. She continued her career with a new backing band, the Kozmic Blues Band, with which she released the album *I Got Dem Ol' Kozmic Blues Again Mama!* in 1969, and performed at Woodstock, leaving her mark at the pivotal rock festival of the time. But things began to go badly at Woodstock for fragile Pearl. When she arrived in a helicopter together with her friend Peggy Caserta and Joan Baez, she was frightened by the huge crowd and ran backstage to shoot up heroin. She sang at dawn on 17 August and the enthusiastic audience demanded an encore of *Ball and Chain*. However, Janis found it difficult to stand up and was disappointed with her performance, which was not included in the documentary film of the festival.

In February 1970 a trip to Brazil seemed to have changed the course of her life for the last time. Janis wanted to break free of drugs and alcohol. She had a love story with an American, David Niehaus. "I finally remembered I don't have to be on stage twelve months a year," she said in a *Rolling Stone* interview. "I've decided

to go and dig some other jungles for a couple of weeks." But, unfortunately, that story ended like the others. Janis resumed shooting up heroin as soon as she returned to the United States, David left her and she returned to the stage to give vent to her torment with a new band, the Full Tilt Boogie Band. "I'm a victim of my own insides," she told the journalist David Dalton during the *Festival Express* tour in Canada that she made with the Grateful Dead, The Band and others. In the opinion of many critics that was the high point of her career.

Her final live concert was on 12 August 1970 at the Harvard Stadium in Boston. Immediately afterwards, Janis decided to cut a new album with the Full Tilt Boogie Band and the producer of The Doors, Paul Rothchild. She moved to Hollywood, settling in a historic rock star haunt, the Landmark Hotel. But this was also the haunt of drug pushers, among whom there was a certain George, who was considered to be very reliable. Janis told her heroin companion Peggy Caserta that she was clean, but it wasn't true. She merely looked a little more attractive, was eager to resume her music-

making and was happy in her relationship with new love Seth Morgan, who was waiting for her in the San Francisco Bay Area. However, she continued her drug consumption and was overwhelmed by the death of Jimi Hendrix. Peggy Caserta told her not to worry: "Two rock stars can't die the same year." That was a terrible prophesy. On 4 October 1970 Janis did not show up at the scheduled rehearsal with her band at the Sunset Sound Recorders studio. The road manager of the Full Tilt Boogie Band, John Cooke, went to the Landmark Hotel to find her. Her car, a Porsche Cabriolet painted in psychedelic colours, was in the hotel parking lot. John went into her room and found Janis dead, lying between her bed and the bedside table. Sixteen days had passed since Jimi Hendrix's death. Janis Joplin was also only 27 years old.

What had happened that last night? Didn't Janis want to break free from heroin? On 3 October she had been in the recording studio for the last time to listen to the instrumental track of a new song, *Buried Alive in the Blues*. She had spent the evening in Barney's Beanery in Los Angeles, where she drank a couple of cocktails with her keyboardist Ken Pearson. She went back to the hotel early and went out only to buy some cigarettes. The rest is mystery. Only one thing is certain: the heroin that George had sold her a few days before was pure and, thus, much more potent than usual. The coroner's verdict leaves no room for doubt: Janis Joplin died of an overdose. Her ashes were scattered over the Pacific Ocean, from an airplane. A few months later, on 11 January 1971, her final album, which was her greatest success, was released: the title was *Pearl*.

44 and 45 On 4 June 1966 Janis Joplin joined Big Brother and the Holding Company. They debuted at the Avalon Ballroom in San Francisco. Here she is with the Full Tilt Boogie Band in 1970.

46 and 47 During her career Janis Joplin won three gold certifications: the first was with Big Brother and the Holding Company for *Cheap Thrills*, the second was with the Kozmic Blues Band for *I Got Dem Ol' Kozmic Blues Again Mama!* and the third (posthumous) was with the Full Tilt Boogie Band for *Pearl*. Her cover of Kris Kristofferson's *Me and Bobby McGee* topped the American charts after her death.

"PEARL'S LOST"

[World Daily News, Special Edition

48 and 49 A special edition of the *World Daily News* dealt with the loss of the Pearl of Rock, as Janis Joplin was called. The singer is seen here during a 1970 concert. She once said: "On stage I make love to 25,000 people; and then I go home alone."

50-51 6 August 1970: Janis Joplin with her last band, The Full Tilt Boogie Band, on stage at the Festival For Peace in Shea Stadium, New York.

JIM MORRISON

"Sometimes... I like to think of the history of rock & roll like the origin of Greek drama. That started out on the threshing floors during the crucial seasons, and was originally a band of acolytes dancing and singing. Then, one day, a possessed person jumped out of the crowd and started imitating a god..." Jim Morrison was not only a singer. His passion was poetry and his greatest aspiration was to make his very life a work of art. In his search for a revolutionary means of expression he chose rock. His literary influences were the Beat generation poets, Baudelaire and William Blake. In 1965 Jim Morrison was in California to escape from a society with which he had nothing in common, and his band, The Doors, took its name from a line in one of Blake's poems: "If the doors of perception were cleansed everything would appear to man as it is, infinite." / "In the universe, there are things that are known, and things that are unknown, and in between, there are doors."

Morrison was the shaman of rock, a poet on loan to music who interpreted the revolutionary aims and needs of his generation as very few others did, an artist who consumed everything in haste to become a myth. He was born in Melbourne, Florida to a very conservative family. His father George Stephen Morrison was an admiral in the U.S. Navy. In 1967, in one of his first interviews Jim said: "You could say it's an accident that I was ideally suited for the work I am doing. It's the feeling of a bow string being pulled back for 22 years and suddenly being let go. [...] I am interested in anything about revolt, disorder, chaos. [...] External freedom is a way to bring about internal freedom."

In 1964, Jim Morrison left Florida and hitched to Los Angeles, where he attended the cinematography course at UCLA, the same one attended by Ray Manzarek, who was the keyboardist in a band called Rick & The Ravens. After graduating, Jim stayed in Los Angeles; he lived on the roof of a house at Venice Beach and spent the summer writing poems, including *Moonlight Drive*. One day Ray met him by chance and Jim sang the first two stanzas to him:

"Let's swim to the moon, let's climb through the tide
Penetrate the evenin', that the city sleeps to hide."

The rest is rock history. Manzarek suggested that they form a band, which they did a short time later, with the arrival of John Densmore, former drummer in Manzarek's band, and Robby Krieger, the guitarist of The Clouds. Their career began by playing gigs in the most notorious club in Los Angeles, London Fog. From a purely musical standpoint those were the years of the stylistic perfection of the Beatles' *Revolver* and the instinctive music of The Doors was a novelty. It was Arthur Lee, of Love, who got them an engagement in the best club in town, Whisky a Go Go. In 1966 The Doors signed with Elektra Records and at the same time lost their job at Whisky a Go Go. Jim Morrison went on stage and sang the acid rock song *The End*, with two lines that left everyone speechless: "Father, I want to kill you, / Mother, I want to [...] you." And so Jim Morrison's first provocation marked the beginning of the band's success.

The band's first album, *The Doors*, was released in 1967; one of its singles, *Light My Fire*, topped the charts and the album sold two million copies. In no time the former Venice Beach drifters became the most important stars on the West Coast and went to live in a villa in Laurel Canyon, while Morrison met his muse, Pamela Courson. The Doors' second album, *Strange Days*, was recorded in the summer of 1967 and their shows became true events. Jim Morrison's fabulous stage presence and the band's furious, "primitive" music created a tension that exploded into mass violence and hysteria. Jim recited poems and acted his role as the Lizard King: "We are from the West. The world we suggest should be of a new wild West, a sensuous, evil world..."

During a 1967 concert in New Haven, Connecticut, Jim Morrison became something more than the vocalist of a famous band: caught by surprise in the dressing room while making love to a girl, he was beaten by a policeman. Later, he went into the audience, found the policeman, began to insult him and was arrested. That incident,

53 "I am interested in anything about revolt, disorder, chaos. It seems to me to be the road toward freedom. External freedom is a way to bring about internal freedom." The intensity of Jim Morrison's words is equal to that of his expression in this 1967 photograph.

documented by a famous journalist from *Life* magazine, caused a sensation. The FBI opened a dossier on him and Jim Morrison became the number one rock 'n' roll rebel, a symbol that became even more powerful during the year when student protests were raging in Berkeley and Paris.

The third chapter of The Doors' story was the album *Waiting for the Sun*. Jim had begun to drink too much and his fellow band members were visibly upset when he was unable to finish a gig or when he provoked the audience. The band regained its former tranquillity during their first European tour and then went back to the studio in 1968 to record their fourth album, *The Soft Parade*. The Doors celebrated its release with the most important concert of their career, Madison Square Garden in New York, but, unfortunately, the band's magic touch was about to end.

The demise of The Doors began in Miami on 1 March 1969, when Morrison was arrested for supposed indecent exposure on stage. The scandal and long trials compromised the band's fame. In 1970 The Doors returned to the recording studio and cut their fifth album, *Morrison Hotel*. However, the Miami trial (in which he was convicted) and the harsh reaction of the establishment powers he had always fought against, began to destroy Morrison. In 1971 The Doors released their sixth album, *L.A. Woman*, which was considered a masterpiece, but it was also Jim's last album. The band wanted to promote it with another tour but managed to play only two dates: the first, in Dallas on 11 December, went smoothly, but the second, at the Warehouse in New Orleans the following day, was a disaster. Morrison collapsed on the stage and refused to sing. John Densmore said he saw Morrison's energy disappear on the stage that night; it was finished, and the band couldn't do anything about it.

When *L.A. Woman* was released Jim Morrison had already left the United States. He went to Paris with Pamela to concentrate on writing poetry. The couple lived in an apartment at 17 rue Beautreillis. Jim shaved off his beard, lost some weight and took long walks with Pamela on the riverside in search of inspiration. But he continued his alcohol and drug consumption. The exception was heroin, which had Pamela firmly in its grip and made her unable to help Jim on his last night, since she was anything but

lucid. It was a night that became one of the great rock mysteries. At 7.30 am on 3 July 1971, Jim was found dead in his bathtub.

The only witness was Pamela, who died of a heroin overdose on 25 April 1974 in her Los Angeles home. Three other people ran to the scene: Count Jean de Breteuil, a French aristocrat who was a drug dealer for rock stars (and who died in Tangiers a few months later at the age of 22), photographer Alain Ronay, and his girlfriend, filmmaker Agnès Varda. No official autopsy was performed and no one saw the corpse, not even The Doors' manager, Bill Siddons, who arrived from America. Manzarek, Krieger and Densmore did not even go to the funeral, which was attended by only five people, in the famous Père Lachaise Cemetery.

There are three different versions of Jim Morrison's death. The first is that he mistakenly sniffed Pamela's heroin, thinking it was cocaine, which caused him to die of internal bleeding. When she woke up from her drugged sleep Pamela found the bathroom door was locked from the inside. She called Jean de Breteuil, who broke the door down and went in: Jim was in the bathtub in a pool of blood, with two purple bruises on his chest. The second version is that Jim never took heroin (which he detested) but had been suffering from serious respiratory problems that were aggravated by his alcohol abuse, and that he died vomiting blood while taking a bath. The third version stems from an interview given in 2007 by a supposed friend of Jim's, Sam Bernett, according to whom Jim died of an overdose in the bathroom of a club on the Left Bank, the Rock and Roll Circus. He had gone there to buy heroin for Pamela, but decided to try some himself in the bathroom. He was then taken to the house on the rue de Beautreillis by the same pushers who had sold him the heroin.

No one knows what really happened. What is certain is that The Doors' music has lived on over the decades as one of the peaks of rock, a brief and intense explosion of creativity that was the concrete expression of its time. Jim Morrison became a myth. His Dionysian spirit, his excesses, his fundamental unhappiness, his overwhelming personality and his talent have been transfigured into the legend of the exemplary rock star, a sex symbol destined for self-destruction who found the path to immortality in his mysterious demise.

56 September 1968: one of Jim Morrison's performances in Frankfurt during the *Waiting for the Sun* European tour.

57 The Doors in a promotional photograph in 1966, at the beginning of their career. From left to right, John Densmore, Robby Krieger, Ray Manzarek and Jim Morrison.

58-59 Jim Morrison in New York (credit Joel Brodsky, 1967) which the photographer named "Jim Morrison, the Young Lion."

KING CURTIS

[7 February 1934 > 13 August 1971]

King Curtis loved music so much that he refused a university scholarship in order to follow his dream. Born in Forth Worth, Texas, Curtis Ousley had begun to play the saxophone at age 12 and soon developed a unique, versatile, syncopated and powerful style that soon led him to concentrate on a new musical genre, rock 'n' roll. In 1952 Curtis arrived in New York and began to work sessions for various rhythm & blues and rock 'n' roll musicians. Success arrived in 1958 when he recorded *Yakety Yak* with the Coasters. His career marked one of the most important convergences of soul and rock. King Curtis played with Buddy Holly, with Aretha Franklin's band, the Kingpins, and he also accompanied John Lennon with sax solos in two songs on his album *Imagine*.

King Curtis was a true musical giant as well being an institution at Atlantic Records, with whom he had worked from 1965. However, one night his extraordinary career came to a tragic end. On 13 August 1971, King Curtis had been returning to his home, an apartment on West 86th Street in New York's Upper West Side. It was a sultry night and he was lugging an air conditioning unit. He saw two junkies using drugs on the steps of the building. When he had asked them to leave, they had refused and an argument ensued which became a fight. King Curtis had had a powerful build, but one of the addicts, 26 year-old Juan Montañez, pulled a knife and stabbed Curtis in the chest. Somehow Curtis managed to pull the weapon out of his chest and stabbed Montañez four times before falling to the ground. He died an hour later at the Roosevelt Hospital. It was one of the many tragic stories that have occurred in the city that never sleeps. We were deprived of one of the greatest musical talents of the 1960s. On the day of his funeral, during which Aretha Franklin sang *Never Grow Old*, Atlantic Records closed its offices. King Curtis was buried in the Pinelawn Memorial Park at Farmingdale, New York, near two other jazz legends, Count Basie and John Coltrane.

60-61 King Curtis at the Montreux Jazz Festival on 12 June 1971. His first success was *Yakety Yak*, a rock 'n' roll piece recorded with the Coasters in 1958. In 1965 Curtis began to lead Aretha Franklin's band, The Kingpins.

DUANE

ALLMAN

In the opinion of many, Duane Allman was the second best guitarist in the world after Jimi Hendrix. In a very short time, the sound made by his Gibson Les Paul, amplified by two 50-watt Marshalls, became a point of reference on the blues scene. Wilson Pickett, who recorded the cover of the Beatles' *Hey Jude* with Allman, called him "Skydog." By the age of 24 Duane Allman had already become a legend. But, in the blues world there is another, disturbing legend, that of the crossroad in the southern United States where Robert Johnson met the devil and sold his soul in order to be a gifted musician. That was the origin of the entire history of the blues. The devil is always waiting at the crossroad, ready to exact his tribute. And one day, in 1971, he took Skydog.

Duane Allman was born in Nashville, Tennessee, the son of a US Army sergeant who was murdered by a hitchhiker that he had given a lift to. Duane grew up in Daytona Beach, Florida but often went back to Nashville to spend a vacation with his grandmother and his younger brother Gregg. It was there that the two discovered music by listening to a neighbour playing country music on his front porch. Duane immediately revealed incredible talent. His mother bought him a Gibson Les Paul Junior and he would lock himself in his bedroom and play nonstop for hours and hours. One day the two brothers went to a B.B. King concert in Nashville. Gregg related that, a few days later, Duane was already able to play all of King's songs as well as improvise solos to them. He was only 13 and had already discovered the blues. In 1965 Gregg and Duane formed their first band, the Allman Joys, and began a long stint on the road performing in clubs in the South. In 1967 they moved to the Promised Land of rock, Los Angeles, and formed a band they called Hour Glass, opening for bands such as The Doors and Buffalo Springfield. They also played, for the first time, at the

Fillmore in San Francisco and recorded two albums, *The Hour Glass* and *Power of Love*. But things didn't work out: their label, Liberty Records, tried to promote them as a pop rock band, but Gregg and Duane wanted to play blues and when playing live they did mostly covers of Otis Redding and the Yardbirds. Duane had already learned, by himself, as always, to play the slide guitar like no one else. In order to get back to playing blues, he went to a legendary recording venue, FAME Studios at Muscle Shoals, Alabama. His guitar lead on the Wilson Pickett album *Hey Jude,* recorded in 1968, was a revelation: the producer of Atlantic Records, Jerry Wexler, wanted him to play sessions on the albums of his most important artists, including Aretha Franklin, King Curtis, Boz Scaggs and Percy Sledge.

But Duane wanted to form his own band and realise his dream of playing the Fillmore East in New York. He began to play with various musicians on the blues and rhythm & blues scene and, in 1969, called his brother Gregg, who had remained in California with The Hour Glass, and told him he had found just the right people for the new band: bass guitarist Berry Oakley, guitarist Dickey Betts and drummers/percussionists Butch Trucks and Jay "Jaimoe" Johanson. That was the birth of the Allman Brothers Band, the architects of Southern Rock. In only two years the band laid the foundation for white blues and went down in history. Between 1969 and 1970 they recorded their first albums, *The Allman Brothers Band* and *Idlewild South,* then Duane met another great blues talent, Eric Clapton, who had wanted to meet him ever since he had heard him play Wilson Pickett's *Hey Jude.* The occasion happened in Miami in 1970: Eric Clapton was recording his album *Layla and Other Assorted Songs* and went to hear an Allman Brothers Band concert, after which he invited Duane to play with him in a long

63 In 2003 *Rolling Stone* magazine chose Duane Allman as the second best guitarist in the history of rock, behind Jimi Hendrix. His nickname, Skydog, was given to him by Wilson Pickett in 1968.

night jam session and then in the studio with him. *Layla and Other Assorted Songs* was an epoch-making album that marked the meeting of two of the best interpreters of blues guitar. But it was also Eric Clapton's cursed album – the desperate howl of grief over his impossible love for the wife of his friend George Harrison, Patty Boyd – which led some of the musicians who cut the album to a tragic fate. Yet another curse loomed over Duane Allman, who, however, in the meantime had seen his dream come true. On 12/13 March 1971 the Allman Brothers Band played the Fillmore East in New York and also cut a double album, *At Fillmore East*, which became one of the most important live albums in the history of rock. It was released in July 1971, but only few months later destiny (or perhaps the devil) ended the life of Duane Allman at a crossroad in the Deep South.

On 29 October Duane was riding his Harley Davidson Sportster motorcycle in Macon, Georgia. He was on his way to the birthday party of Candace Oakley, the sister of Allman Brothers Band bass guitarist Berry Oakley. He was driving fast, way over the speed limit. At the intersection of Hillcrest and

64 The Allman Brothers Band in front of the Rose Hill Cemetery in Macon, Georgia, in 1969. From left to right, Jay "Jaimoe" Johanson, Berry Oakley, Butch Trucks, Duane Allman, Dicky Betts and Gregg Allman. Oakley and Allman are buried in this cemetery.

Bartlett Avenue, a flatbed truck transporting a huge crane was making a left turn. The collision made the motorcycle fly over the intersection. Thus, the curse came to pass: Duane Allman died a few weeks before his 25th birthday.

Berry Oakley was following him in a car, but turned at the preceding crossroad and did not see the accident. He was devastated by his friend's death and often told his friends that the fire had burned out in him. A year later, on 11 November 1972, Berry also met his fate. He too was riding a motorcycle, a Triumph, along the streets of Macon. Alongside him on another motorcycle was a member the Allman Brothers Band crew. They

were playing at chasing one another, but Berry was not a skilful rider. At the Inverness and Napier intersection, he crashed into a bus, going in the opposite direction, and was thrown from the bike. At first it did not seem to be anything serious. He got up and asked to be driven home. Three hours later he was feeling terrible, became delirious and was in a state of confusion. He was taken to the hospital, where the doctors found he had a fractured skull. He died a few hours later. The intersection where his accident occurred is only three blocks away from the one where Duane Allman lost his life. Was that a coincidence or the curse of the blues?

65 Duane Allman during a 1960 concert. Speaking of this fine guitarist, Eric Clapton said: "I remember hearing Wilson Pickett's *Hey Jude* and just being astounded by the lead break at the end. [...] I had to know who that was immediately – right now." According to legend, it was Duane Allman who wrote the opening riff for Derek & The Dominos' *Layla*.

RON McKERNAN

[8 September 1945 > 8 March 1973]

He was called "Pigpen," after the wonderful character in *Peanuts*, since his appearance was not exactly "respectable." Ron McKernan was the son of a Rhythm & Blues DJ in San Bruno, California, so it was only natural that he should grow up with a sound that led him straight to blues and alcohol at a very early age. Word has it that it was "Pigpen" who introduced Janis Joplin to Southern Comfort. The two had a long friendship and a brief relationship. And, like Janis, McKernan also died at age 27. His career in rock music was a kind of illumination and it began when he was quite young. In fact, he left high school when he was 15, became a biker and spent much of his time in the alternative haunts of the San Francisco Bay Area. He grew up with black music and was a keyboardist, drummer and vocalist. In 1961 he met Jerry Garcia at the Boar's Head, a club above a bookstore in San Carlos, California. At the time he was only 16, but his spirit and his blues voice impressed Garcia so much that he asked him to join his band, the Zodiacs. That marked the beginning of a friendship and fellowship that lasted for the entire 1960s: the Zodiacs became the Mother McCree's Uptown Jug Champions with the arrival of Bob Weir, then the Warlocks with the addition of Phil Lesh and Bill Kreutzmann, and then the band changed its name to the Grateful Dead. Ron McKernan was the soul of the band, the first to lead the Grateful Dead from folk to electric rock, the voice of legendary songs like *Turn On Your Love Light*, of which they played a 48 minute version at the Woodstock festival. McKernan was also the only Grateful Dead member who did not experiment with LSD. Until the very end, he remained faithful to Southern Comfort and Thunderbird wine.

In 1971 he was hospitalized for biliary cirrhosis and physicians advised him to stop touring with the band, so he was replaced by pianist Keith Godchaux. "Pigpen" rejoined the Grateful Dead on their 1972 European tour but his health deteriorated markedly. His final concert with the band was on 17 June 1972 at the Hollywood Bowl. On 8 March 1973 he was found dead in his home at Corte Madera, Marin County. The cause of his death was gastrointestinal haemorrhage caused by alcohol abuse.

That marked the beginning of an incredible curse that struck the Grateful Dead keyboardists: Keith Godchaux died on 23 July 1980 in an automobile accident. His replacement, Brent Mydland, died of an overdose on 26 July 1990. And the band's final keyboardist, Vince Welnik, committed suicide in 2006.

66-67 An intense portrait of Ron McKernan, the soul of the Grateful Dead. His most important contribution may have been *Turn On Your Lovelight*. At Woodstock the Grateful Dead played a version of the song that lasted 48 minutes.

GRAM
PARSONS

He called it Cosmic American Music. It was his music, a mixture of blues, folk and psychedelic rock, a drug-ridden journey to the origins of sound. Gram Parsons is one of the unknown heroes of 1960s rock music, the best friend of Keith Richards of the Rolling Stones and his psychedelic trip companion, an inveterate hippy who wanted to be buried in the mystical heart of the Joshua Tree National Park, the site that had inspired his generation. He had also been a blend of country and rock; a pivotal figure on The Byrds' *Sweetheart of the Rodeo* and the author of an even more moving and painful version of The Rolling Stones' *Wild Horses* and the brain of the Flying Burrito Brothers, which enjoyed no commercial success but had a strong influence on American music in subsequent decades. His story is one of the most fascinating in rock history.

Gram Parsons came from a wealthy family: his mother, Avis Connor, had been the daughter of a citrus fruit magnate and his father, Ingram Cecil (whose nickname was "Coon Dog"), had been a highly decorated Second World War flying ace. Gram had been an only child, born in Winter Haven, Florida and christened Ingram Cecil Connor III, a boy whose life was marred at an early stage. His father had committed suicide just two days before Christmas in 1958. His mother later married Robert Parsons, but later she became an alcoholic and died, of cirrhosis,

on 5 July 1965, the very day that Gram had graduated from the prestigious Bolles School in Jacksonville, Florida. Those two events had been a terrible blow for him. Yet he continued to pursue an academic career and attended Harvard University.

There had been a particular moment which marked a turning point in his life. When he was only 10 years old he had discovered rock 'n' roll at an Elvis Presley concert, in Waycross, Georgia, on 22 February 1956. By the age of 15 he was already playing in cover bands in Georgia clubs owned by his stepfather. A year later, at 16, he made the switch to folk music and formed The Shilos and joined the Greenwich Village scene in New York. But it was at Harvard that he had been overwhelmed by country music during a Merle Haggard concert. He only stayed one semester at Harvard and left to form the International Submarine Band, and in 1967 moved to California, where he wrote one of his first, and best-known, songs, *Luxury Liner*. His transformation had been completed: he had become a fully-fledged rock musician. The first person to note that fact was Byrds' bass guitarist Chris Hillman, who took Gram on as the band's pianist to record one of the definitive albums of that time, *Sweetheart of the Rodeo*. During a UK tour with The Byrds, Gram had the second crucial experience of his life: he met the Rolling Stones. During the tour he had left The

Byrds because they had been planning a tour of South Africa and he had had concerns about that country's apartheid policy. He went to stay in Keith Richards' house near Stonehenge, Wiltshire where he introduced Richards to country music and established the beginnings of a close friendship with him. In 1969 Gram, Richards and his girlfriend Anita Pallenberg went on a psychedelic journey in Joshua Tree National Park, in California. That experience united the two musicians for the rest of their lives. Keith Richards related that Gram had the largest repertoire of country songs one could have imagined. "He didn't sell many disks, but his effect on country music is enormous and this is why we we're talking about him now." He added that it had been a pity we would never know what his real impact on future music might have been.

Parsons met Chris Hillman in Los Angeles and formed a new band with him, the Flying Burrito Brothers. In 1969 the band released its debut album, *The Gilded Palace of Sin*, which was promoted with a cross-country railroad tour that had been a true rock 'n' roll adventure, consisting of interminable poker games and the consumption of hallucinogens and cocaine. The album did not sell well but became a landmark in American popular music. The band almost went bankrupt, and the Rolling Stones tried, in vain, to help Gram by inviting the Burritos to be one

69 Gram Parsons jokes with the photographer during a photo session in 1969. He was a member of three bands: The International Submarine Band, the Byrds and the Flying Burrito Brothers. His "cosmic American music" influenced generations of musicians, from Keith Richards through Emmylou Harris to Elvis Costello.

of the acts in the Altamont Festival. The Flying Burrito Brothers then released a second album, *Burrito Deluxe*, but that was not been a success either.

Gram Parsons was a great rock musician who never became a rock star. In 1971 he accompanied the Rolling Stones on the trip that led to the creation of their album *Exile on Main Street*. In order to break loose from the grip of the British taxation system, the Stones had taken refuge at Villafranche-sur-Mer, on the French Riviera, and had set up a recording studio in Keith Richards' home, Villa Necôte. Along with the musicians were their girlfriends, various drug dealers and many friends, including William Burroughs, Marshall Chess, Bobby Keys and Gram. And there was plenty of heroin, which loomed over the lives of Keith Richards and his friend Gram. In July 1971 the French police began to become interested in what was happening at the villa and Anita Pallenberg had asked Gram to leave. According to rumours he sang in the chorus of the Stones' *Sweet Virginia*.

From that time Parsons' life deteriorated. He released his solo album *GP* (1973), went on tour with Emmylou Harris and also tried to kick his heroin addiction several times. He put on a lot of weight, caused a fire that totally destroyed his Topanga Canyon home, leaving intact only one guitar and his Jaguar automobile, and began a secret relationship with an old school friend, Margaret Fisher. And he became more and more

enamoured of the magical Joshua Tree National Park, where he would spend days on end on psychedelic trips. In fact, one day he asked his friend and road manager Phil Kaufman to bury him in Joshua Tree if he should die. "As far as drugs and alcohol are concerned, Gram was no better or worse than the rest of us," Keith Richards once stated. "He only went a step further."

On 17 September 1973, Gram went to Joshua Tree. He had just finished recording his second solo album, *Grievous Angel*, and wanted to relax and enjoy a good time. He had been accompanied by Margaret Fisher, his assistant Michael Martin and Michael's girlfriend Dale. The vacation in the Joshua Tree Inn had immediately turned into a delirious experience: Michael Martin had had to return to Los Angeles to purchase some more marijuana, Gram had begun drinking whisky and had managed to get hold of a large amount of morphine. He passed out and had to be re-animated by Margaret, who then went out, leaving Gram alone with Dale. When Margaret returned she found that Gram had passed out again. An ambulance took him to the Hi-Desert Memorial Hospital, but he was pronounced dead upon his arrival.

Another legend: Gram had taken enough morphine to kill three people. But the truth about his death is still an open question. The police did not really question Margaret and Dale, nor did they write an official report, because, in the meantime, Phil Kaufman had

arrived at Joshua Tree, where he had removed all the drugs from Gram's room and had quickly taken the two women back to Los Angeles. He had also decided to keep the promise he had made to his friend. Gram Parsons had been heir to a large estate. His stepfather Robert Parsons had wanted to take his body to Louisiana and organise a private funeral without inviting any of Gram's musician friends – perhaps in an effort to get hold of his legacy, to which he could lay valid claim. The coffin was already at Los Angeles airport, about to be put on a plane headed for Louisiana, when Kaufman and Martin arrived. They had been drunk but, incredibly enough, somehow managed to convince people at the airport that they were employees of the family's funeral parlour and they took their friend's coffin, in a borrowed hearse, and headed for Cap Rock, the spot in the Joshua Tree Park where Gram had said he had wanted to be buried. Once there, Phil and Michael initiated a surreal cremation ceremony: they tossed gasoline on the corpse, inside the coffin, and set it alight. Gram Parsons' dream had come true: his soul wandered in the Joshua Tree Park desert. His remains now lie in a New Orleans cemetery, in a tomb on which is carved the title of one of his songs: *God's Own Singer*. Kaufman and Martin received incredibly light punishment: a fine of 750 dollars for having damaged the coffin, since stealing a corpse was not a crime in California. They had kept their promise.

71 The Flying Burrito Brothers in 1969 on the release of their debut album, *The Gilded Palace of Sin*. Although it sold only a few thousand copies, it is considered to be a fundamental country rock album.

MAMA CASS

[19 September 1941 > 29 July 1974]

She was the symbol of the Summer of Love: live freely, play freely, love freely. It was a positive, bright philosophy that represented the ideals of the 1960s and the California hippy lifestyle. Mama Cass (also known as Cass Elliot) was the vocalist of the Mamas & Papas. Born Ellen Naomi Cohen, in Baltimore, she was a major figure in the history of American rock and her voice and impressive stage presence left her mark on the golden decade of music. Her life ended in 1974, just when she had decided not to be Mama Cass any longer.

Her career began in the early 1960s, in the Greenwich Village folk scene. Mama Cass worked as a cloakroom attendant in The Showplace club while, in the meantime, acting in the musical *The Music Man* and also singing in a folk group called The Triumvirate. In 1963 the band changed its name to The Big Three (the other members were Tim Rose and James Hendricks) and debuted with a new interpretation of a famous children's poem, *Winkin', Blinkin' and Nod*. For a year the Big Three were riding high: they played at the Bitter End club, recorded two albums and some commercials, and also experimented with pop-folk. However, in 1964 Tim Rose left the band and Cass, together with James Hendricks, Zal Yanovsky and Denny Doherty, formed the Mugwumps, a band that lasted only eight months but which spawned two of the pillars of 1960s rock music, The Mamas & Papas and Lovin' Spoonful. The pieces of this musical puzzle came together in 1964: Doherty formed a trio with John Phillips and his wife Michelle, The New Journeymen; Yanovsky joined Lovin' Spoonful; Cass went to sing in Washington D.C. jazz clubs. One day Doherty persuaded Phillips to go hear her sing. Her voice left him speechless. They all left together on a trip to the Virgin Islands and after a few weeks of experimentation with acid and vocal melodies, a period when they spent all their money, they decided to try their luck in the Promised Land of rock, California.

It was 1965 and the band changed its name to The Mamas & Papas. When they arrived in Los Angeles they wrote a song, *California Dreamin'*, which epitomised the era. It was released in November 1965 and went unnoticed at first until a Boston radio station began to broadcast it non-stop. The delightful melodic structure of the piece and its description of a winter day's walk, while dreaming of the California sun, became part and parcel of the collective imagination of a generation, and *California Dreamin'* peaked at number four in the 1966 American charts. The Mamas & Papas then released *If You Can Believe Your Eyes and Ears*, which topped the charts and helped organise and then close the Monterey Pop Festival, the first great event of the Summer of Love. However, there were the beginnings of disharmony in the band. When they arrived in California, The Mamas & Papas were innocent and full of ideals; they were four young people happy to sing and play together. John Phillips was the singer-songwriter, the author of the band's bright and cheerful sound; Denny Doherty was the fascinating soloist and Michelle Phillips a stunning beauty. And Mama Cass was Mother Nature to the hippy universe, with a huge heart and a legendary voice.

72 and 73 30 July 1974: the front page of *The Sun* newspaper with news of Cass Elliott's death. Her voice epitomised the 1960s Summer of Love.

But in 1969 things had already changed. The Vietnam War was stifling the hippy dream, the Summer of Love was over, and The Mamas & Papas were torn by bitter arguments and betrayals, by too much free love and too many free drugs. The secret relationship between Doherty and Michelle led to the band splitting up and being formed anew in 1966, and an argument between John Phillips and Cass Elliot transformed the recording sessions of the band's fourth album into mere contractual obligations. The Mamas & Papas disbanded just like the hopes for change of an entire generation.

Mama Cass made her debut as a solo artist in 1968 with the album *Dream a Little Dream*, which was followed by *Bubblegum, Lemonade and... Something for Mama* (1969) and *Mama's Big Ones* (1971), three albums she had trouble finishing in time due to the pressing schedule of her contract with Dunhill Records. Moreover, the albums did not enjoy much success. Cass Elliot wanted to be free of her stage name, Mama, and no longer wanted to be the hippies' voice-symbol. By now her relationship with her old band had ended. Only Michelle Phillips remained close; in fact, after Cass died she also helped her daughter Owen Vanessa Elliot, born on 16 April 1967, to find her biological father.

Cass signed a contract with RCA and released two more albums, *Cass Elliot* and *The Road Is No Place For a Lady*, but again success eluded her. It was only when she met Allan Carr, the manager of Peter Sellers and Tony Curtis, that a turning point in her career finally arrived. Carr brought Cass back to the theatre and introduced her to the world of cabaret with the show *Don't Call Me Mama Anymore*, which debuted on 9 February 1973 in Pittsburgh and went on to be a huge success in Las Vegas. Her voice shone once again, and the transformation seemed complete! Cass Elliot was no longer Mama Cass. In July 1974 she flew to London for a series of sell-out concerts at the London Palladium. She stayed at the Mayfair apartment of a friend, singer Harry Nilsson, at 9 Curzon Place. On 28 July she phoned Michelle. In tears, she described the triumphant reception she had had, the public's ovation, the thrill of, again, feeling she was a great artist. The following day she was found dead, at the age of 32. The official cause of death was a heart attack caused by her obesity and heart problems. No traces of alcohol or drugs were found in her system: Mama Cass was clean and ready to make her comeback. The voice that was the symbol of the 1960s died in her sleep.

NICK DRAKE

[19 June 1948 > 25 November 1974]

77 Nick Drake released three albums from 1969 to 1972: *Five Leaves Left*, *Bryter Layter* and *Pink Moon*. In one single in *Five Leaves Left*, *Fruit Tree*, he sings: "Life is but a memory/ Happened long ago/Theatre full of sadness/For a long forgotten show."

Five Leaves Left. Five leaves left on the tree, five years to understand the mystery of one of the most enigmatic singer-songwriters in English music – a tragic story of a person whose life seemed to be doomed. In fact, Nick Drake made his debut in 1969 with *Five Leaves Left* and died only five years later, at his home in Tanworth-in-Arden, Warwickshire, of an overdose of a prescribed anti-depressant. It may have been an accident or it may have been the gesture of a desperate soul who suffered from insomnia and depression. Drake released only three albums, *Five Leaves Left*, *Bryter Layter* and *Pink Moon*, none of which sold more than 5,000 copies. He did not like to be interviewed and felt ill at ease performing live but his delicate, poetic songs eventually became historic and influenced English music in later years.

Nick Drake was born in Rangoon, Burma; his father was an engineer and his mother the daughter of a British Army officer. He had a sister, Gabrielle, who became an actress. When Nick was two years old his family moved to Tanworth-in-Arden, Warwickshire. There he began to learn piano and guitar, influenced by his mother Molly who was a singer-songwriter with a style much like the one that would be the signature sound of her son. Nick was an introverted, timid, withdrawn person. "None of us really knew him," his father Rodney stated. But, as a youth, he was filled with vitality and had a passion for life and writing music. Nobody really knows what happened to him inwardly. In 1965 he bought his first guitar and began to show more interest in music than in his studies. Before going

up to Cambridge University he spent six months at a French university, discovered LSD and marijuana (which he consumed in large quantities during the rest of his life) and also devoured the music of Bob Dylan and began to play in London folk music clubs. In 1968 he was noticed when he opened for Country Joe and The Fish at the Roundhouse in London and met the person who would become his manager, producer and good friend for the rest of his brief career, Joe Boyd. In fact, Boyd got him a recording contract after listening to a demo tape of four songs Nick had recorded in his room in Cambridge. His first album, *Five Leaves Left*, was released on 1 September 1969 but was ignored by the critics. Nick was dissatisfied with the production, the insert sleeve (which contained mistakes) and the promotion of the album. The following year he left Cambridge and went to London to concentrate on making his way in the music world. But live performances disappointed him more and more. He could not appreciate the folk music scene, was reluctant to communicate with the audience and spent a long time tuning his guitar before each song.

1970 saw the release of his second album, *Bryter Layter*, in which he played with some members of Fairport Convention and also collaborated with John Cale. But the album was received coldly and sold less than 3,000 copies. In the meantime Joe Boyd had moved to Los Angeles, leaving Nick feeling more alone than ever. He fell into a deep depression. A physician prescribed anti-depressants for the first time, but Nick continued to smoke marijuana while taking the

medicine and isolated himself more and more in his London home. His sister Gabrielle said later that it was from that moment that things started to go wrong for Nick. However, he managed to cut a new album, *Pink Moon*, for guitar and voice, that was recorded in only two two-hour sessions in October 1971. The album got some good reviews but sold even fewer than his preceding albums. However, it became a cult album among his fans.

From that time Drake decided to withdraw from music. He was extremely disappointed with the London scene and angry about the lack of consideration on the part of the press and public alike. He was a 20 year-old with a radical, artistic spirit and a soul that was fragile and too sensitive and he was tragically aware of having arrived at a dead end. In 1971 Nick returned to live with his parents where he managed to survive on the 20 pounds a week he received from his record label, Island Records. His behaviour became more and more bizarre. At times he would drive for hours in the Warwickshire countryside until he had no fuel left and had to call his parents and have them fetch him. At other times he would surprise friends in London by showing up at their homes without warning; he would sit in a corner without uttering a word, stay there for days on end and leave in silence. Nick Drake was a tormented genius who always felt less and less understood, a tragic figure who left us beautiful songs with a strong feeling of sadness about the dramatic mysteries of the human psyche. His illness conditioned his life more drastically from 1972. His only 'romantic' relationship, with his friend Sophia Ryde, ended a few weeks before his death.

However, it seemed that music might have offered him one last way out of his plight: in February 1974 Nick said that he was ready to record another album. He asked for help from Joe Boyd, who had returned from America. The recording sessions were extremely difficult but Nick seemed to have regained some of his former enthusiasm. He then went to France to see some friends, coming back in high spirits that his family had not seen in his eyes for years. He told them he felt better and wanted to go back to London to resume his career. That may have been the reason why he committed a fatal error one night when he could not sleep. A doctor had prescribed an anti-depressant called Amitriptyline (Tryptizol). On the night of 24 November 1974 Nick went to bed early, which was unusual. At around dawn he got up to have a snack in the kitchen, something he did so often that his family paid no attention to it. Nor were they concerned because he had not yet got up by noon that day. When his mother Molly finally went into his bedroom she found him lying on his bed. He was dead: cardiac arrest brought about by an overdose of Amitriptyline. The medical report stated that he had died at 6.00 am. After his snack, Nick had gone back to his bedroom, taken a large number of pills, in order to sleep, and this had proven to be fatal. Or, he may have committed suicide, since he seemed to have given up on life a long time before. The only thing we know for sure is that he was 26. Carved on the headstone of his grave, which lies under a tree in St. Mary's Cemetery, Tanworth-in-Arden, is a verse from *From the Morning*, the last song on *Pink Moon*: "Now we rise/ And we are everywhere."

TIM
BUCKLEY

[14 February 1947 > 29 June 1975]

Tim Buckley was a model student in high school. He played baseball and was the football team quarterback. But, at a certain point, he began to develop other interests – folk music and beat poetry. He had learned to play the banjo when he was 13 and often played in public with his buddy Dan Gordon. He was a restless, anxiety-ridden soul. A sensation of being 'inadequate for life' always accompanied him. He broke two fingers of his left hand during a football game and he abandoned the sport. He also lost interest in school and set out to devote his energy to art and music. That was a way of keeping his distance from his father, a highly decorated World War Two veteran, who had become violent and unstable. During his last two years at high school, part of which he spent at Loara High School in Anaheim, he played music and recited poetry with two folk bands, The Bohemians and The Harlequin 3, and he met fellow student Mary Guibert, who soon became pregnant.

They married on 25 October 1965, when Tim was only 18. "I'll give you three months at the most," his father had told him. And, in truth, marriage and fatherhood were too much for him. Tim could not cope and he and Mary divorced in October 1966, one month after the birth of their son, Jeff Buckley. He left Fullerton College after only two weeks to dedicate his life to music. "And I can't swim your waters / And you can't walk my lands / I'm sailing all my sins / And I'm climbing all my fears / And soon now I'll fly," he wrote in a song dedicated to Mary, *I Never Asked To Be Your*

Mountain. Tim played in the folk clubs of Los Angeles, including the one managed by his friend Dan Gordon.

In February 1966 he went to live in the Bowery neighbourhood of New York with his new girlfriend, Jainie Goldstein, to realise his dreams. He was discovered by Mothers of Invention manager Herb Cohen, who got him a contract with Elektra Records and, in 1966, Tim made his debut album, *Tim Buckley*. But he was not satisfied with it. He didn't like the result, he wanted something more and the following year he released an album of poetry and music entitled *Goodbye and Hello*. Elektra Records attempted to launch him by having him participate in the *Tonight Show*, but Tim refused to lip-sync and had an argument with the host. He wasn't at all interested in the charts and couldn't tolerate the rules of the music business, since his aim was to use music only as a means to express his creativity. His career was a series of continuous experimentation that, at first, attracted but then disorientated his fans, who ended up criticising him. Tim Buckley's music is folk, rock, free jazz and avant-garde and, at the same time, none of those. He was a cult musician and a poet idolised by only a small public. His most popular album, *Happy Sad*, released in 1968, only reached number 81 in the charts. A year later he reacted to that by recording material for three totally experimental albums, *Lorca*, *Blue Afternoon* and *Starsailor*, which came out one after another but were commercial flops and left him virtually penniless. Tim Buckley then

fell victim to alcohol and drug dependence, while at the same time attempting to regain success with three more albums, *Greetings from L.A.*, *Sefronia* and *Look at the Fool*, but, unfortunately, they did not attract notice.

In 1975 he seemed to have found his way out of his dire situation. He had stopped taking drugs and had announced his comeback with a tour and a live album. But his tormented spirit got the better of him. On 18 June 1975 Tim Buckley ended the tour with a sold out show in Dallas and began to drink. The following day he was drunk and went to the home of his friend Richard Keeling, to get some heroin. The two had an argument and Richard handed him a large dose, telling him to take it all and get out. Tim snorted a large amount and went home. When his wife, Judy, arrived she found him unconscious. She put him to bed and went to phone friends and the band members in an attempt to understand what had happened. When she came back to the bedroom he was dead. He was 28, and at that moment a guitar and amplifier were all that he owned. Richard Keeling was accused of manslaughter and sentenced to four months in prison and four years of probation.

Had Tim Buckley managed to break free from the drug habit he could still have produced memorable music. His two posthumous live albums *Dream Letter* and *Live at the Troubadour 1969* are proof of that. His talent survived in his son, whom he met only once, Jeff Buckley, who, sadly, also seemed to walk his father's tragic pathway.

79 During his career Tim Buckley, seen here during a 1968 performance, explored many musical genres, including folk, jazz and psychedelia. His guitarist, Lee Underwood, once said: "Tim had an exceptional voice that ranged between the baritone and tenor registers. What is more important, he knew exactly what to do with it."

ELVIS

[8 January 1935 > 16 August 1977]

PRESLEY

"The king is gone but he's not forgotten," Neil Young sang in *My My Hey Hey (Out to Blue)* released in 1979, "[...] rock and roll can never die." The death of the King, Elvis Presley, had been an unprecedented event, just like his life. Elvis Presley died the morning of 16 August 1977 at Graceland, his villa in Memphis, Tennessee. He was just 42 years old. A huge crowd gathered in front of his home and many fans, in search of news, went to the Baptist Memorial Hospital where Elvis had been taken by two members of his crew, the so-called Memphis Mafia, after having been found unconscious by his girlfriend Ginger Alden. The news was released officially at 3.30 pm. One of the most important icons of the 20th century, the very symbol of rock 'n' roll, had gone forever. His funeral was a ceremony fit for a head of state: a procession of 17 white Cadillacs had moved between two rows of people, toward the Forest Hills Cemetery in Memphis. American president Jimmy Carter issued the following statement about Presley: "His music and his personality, fusing the styles of white country and black rhythm and blues, permanently changed the face of American popular culture." One of Elvis's cousins, Billy Mann, accepted 18,000 dollars to take a photograph of the corpse. The photo ended up on the front cover of the *National Enquirer's* biggest selling issue ever. Elvis had then been taken back to Graceland to be buried near his mother Gladys Love, so everything had ended where it had begun.

On 18 July 1953, when Elvis had entered a recording studio for the first time (Sun Records, in Memphis), it had been to record an acetate disk as a birthday present for his mother. He had paid nearly four dollars to cut two sides with the songs

My Happiness / That's When Your Heartaches Begin. The studio receptionist Marion Keisker had asked Elvis what type of music he sang, and he, who at the time was a truck driver, replied: "I sing all kinds." He returned on 4 January 1954 to record another acetate, *I'll Never Stand In Your Way / It Wouldn't Be the Same Without You.* The producer, Sam Phillips, had been looking for a white singer with an African-American voice so Marion Keisker reminded him about the truck driver from Tupelo and was told to call him on 26 May 1954 for an audition. On 5 July Elvis recorded his first single for Sun Records, *That's All Right Mama,* a cover of a blues song by Arthur Crudup, accompanied by Scotty Moore on guitar and Bill Black on double bass. For a long time the three tried various songs and had had no luck finding the right sound. Discouraged, they had decided to take a break. Then Elvis took the microphone and began to improvise a very rhythmic version of *That's all Right Mama.* Bill Black and Scotty Moore perked up and followed him, and Sam Phillips rushed in to record that new sound.

That was the beginning of the King of Rock's great career: 12 albums that topped both country and pop charts, from *Elvis Presley* (1956) to *From Elvis Presley Boulevard, Memphis, Tennessee* (1976); 134 million albums sold; 18 singles going to number one in the charts, from *Heartbreak Hotel* (1956) to *Suspicious Mind* (1969). Charismatic, attractive, with great stage presence, a unique voice and rhythm in his blood, Elvis also became the first 'super star' in show business. He signed a lucrative contract with RCA in 1956 made two TV appearances on the very popular *Ed Sullivan Show* that were viewed by one-third of American families.

That marked the birth of rock as a mass phenomenon in the younger generation, which identified with rock and went crazy over Elvis, who became what could be called a success machine.

But in the meantime, what had been happening to him mentally? Elvis became a contemporary icon partly because he was consumed by success. He transformed himself totally into his persona and was devoured by it, exploited to the utmost by an ever-increasing entourage of unscrupulous friends and relatives, opportunistic collaborators and parasites of all kinds, all of whom were interested only in keeping his kingdom going at all costs. His life as a star was also a continuous series of excess and abuse that ruined the health of a man who was still young and full of talent. Indeed, he was an artist able to make a great comeback when everything seemed to go badly. When the music scene changed with the 1967 Summer of Love, the hippy movement, the Beatles and Jimi Hendrix, the King of Rock remained silent. He had spent two years in military service between 1958 and 1960, then found that his career had reached stalemate. His last number one song in the American charts at that time had been *Good Luck Charm* (1962), and although such legendary songs as *Are You Lonesome Tonight* and *Can't Help Falling in Love* continued to be re-released, his music had become somewhat obscured. His manager, Colonel Tom Parker, had created an acting career for him that brought in one million dollars per movie, and Elvis made 25 movies between 1956 and 1967, all of them panned by the critics. In 1968 the Presley myth seemed to be a mere memory until on 3 December when he starred in the *Comeback Special* TV show. He had not performed live since 1961 and

81 The *Daily Mail* of 17 August 1977 announces Elvis Presley's death in Memphis. The entire front page is given over to the shocking news, with the headline of Presley's death. The amazing success story of The King, seen here in an intense close-up, began in 1956.

82 and 83 Elvis Presley relaxing in his dressing room before a concert in the Oakland Auditorium in June 1956. Opposite page. 16 August 1956: The King is surrounded by enthusiastic fans in Los Angeles who are asking for his autograph.

now, dressed entirely in black leather, he had become fascinating and mysterious. He sang for an hour and in one fell swoop he had conquered the public again. Later, he told producer Steve Binder: "I give you my word, I will never sing a song I don't believe in." Soon afterwards he went to the American Sound Studio in Memphis and recorded his first album in eight years, *From Elvis in Memphis*. He then returned to live performing and just kept on going. He gave 178 concerts in 1973 alone. That was the period of his live shows in Las Vegas, a final scintillating explosion that lasted to the end of his life.

Elvis had begun to consume amphetamines during his military service in Germany and had become an addict. He led a nocturnal life and slept during the day, and his eating habits were simply insane, since he would eat anything. However, his worst habit was the dependency on all kinds of drugs, which his personal physician, George C.

Nichopoulos, prescribed for him. After all, he was the King, he was very wealthy and could have anything he wanted at any time he wanted. But, in the meantime, he had been reduced to mere caricature of his former self. One concert in Alexandria, Louisiana lasted only 30 minutes, and in Baton Rouge he'd been unable to get out of bed to perform. His final concert was held in the Market Square Arena in Indianapolis on 26 June 1977. But the last day of his life, 15 August 1977, was worthy of a king.

He went to his dentist at 10.30 pm and then returned to Graceland. He asked Dr. Nichopoulos to prescribe a painkiller. He had argued with his girlfriend, Ginger, who did not want to go with him on his upcoming tour. Elvis had cancelled some tour concerts but absolutely wanted to go back on stage, despite the fact that his latest shows had been disappointing. The next day a private plane was waiting to take him to Portland, Maine.

At 3.00 am Elvis called his cousin Billy Smith and one of his bodyguards, Joe Esposito, to play squash with him. Then he took some tranquilizers and told Ginger that he was going to the bathroom to read one of his "spiritual" books, *Sex and Psychic Energy* by Betty Bethards. Ginger found him there a few hours later, lying on the floor with his trousers down. The King had died in his bathroom.

The autopsy was conducted by the coroner Jerry Francisco in the presence of other physicians, including Dr. Nichopoulos (whose medical license was later suspended). The medical report was a kind of press release aimed at calming both the press and the public: the cause of death was listed as "cardiac arrhythmia." But the truth was, Elvis had suffered from high blood pressure, glaucoma, had a damaged liver and some serious intestinal problems. And in his system were found several chemical substances well above the maximum level of a normal person, as well as a King.

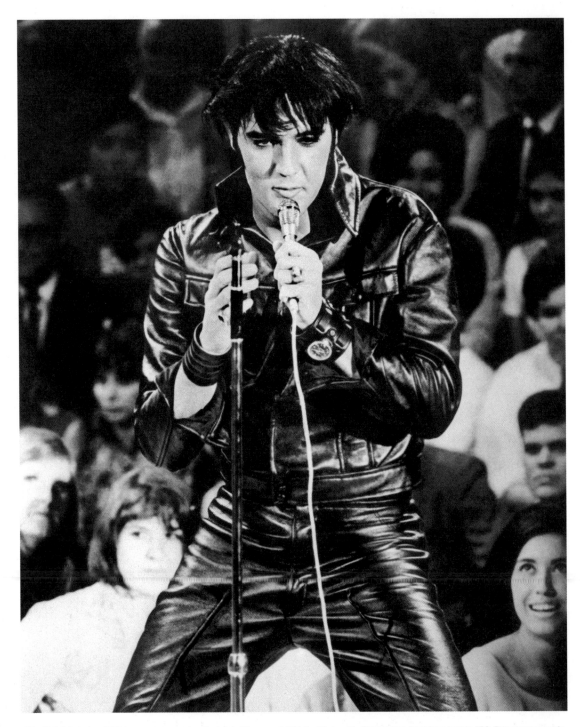

84 and 85 3 December 1968: it was seven years since Presley's last live concert. With the TV show *The '68 Comeback Special* broadcast by NBC, Elvis set out to regain the great success he had enjoyed in the 1950s, when the photograph on the opposite page was taken.

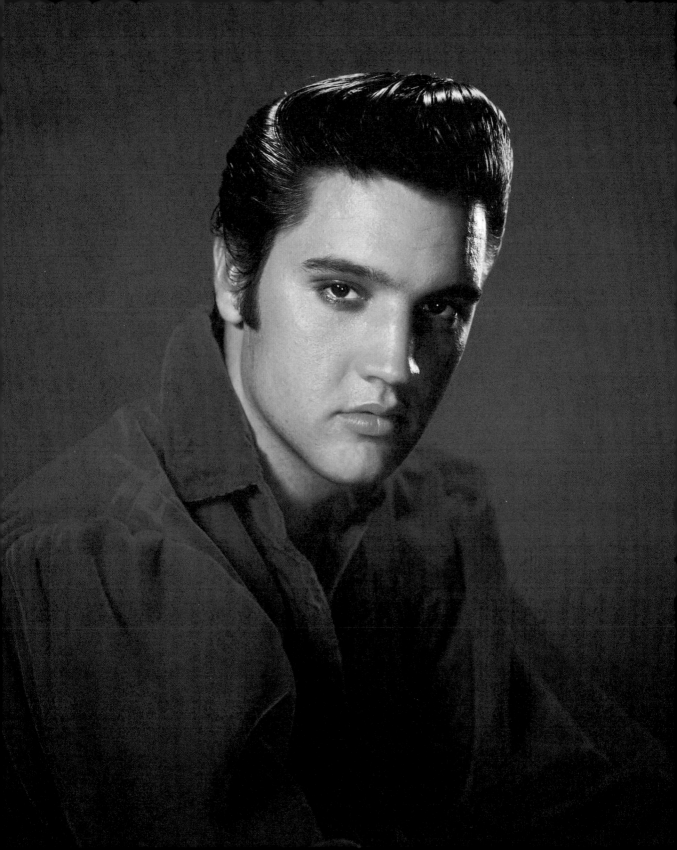

"And Lady Stardust sang his songs of darkness and dismay. [...] And he was awful nice / Really quite out of sight / And he sang all night long." That was how David Bowie described the brilliant star in the glam rock firmament in 1973. *Lady Stardust* was Mark Feld, whose stage name was Marc Bolan, a musician with a scintillating image who became the symbol of an intense period of the British music scene. Glam artists were apparently androgynous, as well as decadent, flamboyant and romantic, and they lived life as a work of art. Their music was a nervous, electric rock filled with ambiguous implications that conquered the British public. That departure from reality was marked by the use of space, ambiguity, and a theatrical sound full of melody. David Bowie was the most famous star on the glam scene, but the genre was inspired by Marc Bolan. Bolan had discovered rock through the likes of Chuck Berry and Eddie Cochran, and had formed a skiffle band when he was still very young. He had then become a mod and made his first TV appearance on the children's TV show *Orlando*. He then made his debut as a singer, having changed his name to Toby Tyler, discovered folk music, changed his name again, to Marc Bolan (some biographers think "Bolan" is an acronym of Bob Dylan), and in 1968 formed an acoustic duo, with Steve Peregrine Took, for which he created a fanciful name, Tyrannosaurus Rex. After four albums and a collection of poems, *The Warlock of Love*, Marc Bolan came to a turning point in his career; he replaced his acoustic guitar with a

MARC BOLAN

[30 September 1947 > 16 September 1977]

Gibson Les Paul, shortened the name of the band to T. Rex and created a new look for himself. He began wearing top hats, paillette glitter on his cheeks (in an interview on BBC Radio 1 he said that he got the idea from his first wife, June Child, who had used glitter), make-up and snakeskin jackets, and now had a new sound, all of which made Bolan's T. Rex the sensation of the moment. The band's first single, *Ride a White Swan*, was released on 9 October 1970. T. Rex gave an historical exhibition on the *Top of the Pops* TV show and the song went to number two in the charts. The band's first album, *T. Rex*, was released in 1971, followed by *Electric Warrior* in 1972 which was number one in the charts for two months. The glam rock star was shining brightly but burned out quickly. The next album, *The Slider*, launched the single *Metal Guru* (which became their fourth consecutive number one after *Hot Love*, *Get It On* and *Telegram Sam*), after which Marc Bolan changed his style once again; while the glam fashion was declining, giving way to the punk revolution, he injected soul and R&B into his rock in *Tanx*, *Zinc Alloy and the Hidden Riders of Tomorrow*, *Bolan's Zip Gun*, *Futuristic Dragon* and *Dandy in the Underworld*. The last-mentioned album heralded the beginning of yet another watershed in his career. He retained the magic of his past glam style yet incorporated punk rock elements of the New Wave. But the story of Lady Stardust ended on 16 September 1977. Marc Bolan and his second wife, Gloria Jones, had left Mortons restaurant in Berkeley Square, London in a purple Mini 1275 GT that Gloria drove (Marc Bolan never had a driving license, since he was afraid of having an accident). While the car was going down Queens Ride in the Barnes area of south London, the Mini went off the road and crashed into a tree. Gloria Jones received a broken jaw and arm but Marc Bolan was killed instantly. He would have turned 30 two weeks later, on 30 September. At his funeral, attended by David Bowie and Rod Stewart among many others, there was a large floral arrangement in the shape of a swan, a tribute to his first hit, *Ride a White Swan*.

87 Marc Bolan in 1976, after his eleventh album, *Futuristic Dragon*, was released. A year later, on 16 September 1977, Bolan died in a car accident in London, two weeks before his 30th birthday. "I live my life with a sense of urgency that most people can't comprehend."

RONNIE
VAN ZANT

[15 January 1948 > 20 October 1977]

STEVE GAINES

[14 September 1949 > 20 October 1977]

1974 was the year of a song that made Southern rock music popular throughout the world. It was sung by Lynyrd Skynyrd and was entitled *Sweet Home Alabama*. The song was a token of love for a place filled with passion and mystery, legends and curses, such as the one that struck the band one night in 1977.

Ronnie Van Zant always told his friends that he would become the most famous citizen of his home town, Jacksonville, Florida. He had wanted to be boxer, a baseball player or a stock-car driver, but on the way he had found rock 'n' roll instead. In 1964 he formed his first band, The Noble Five, with two school friends from the Robert E. Lee High School, Allen Collins and Gary Rossington. The following year Larry Junstrom and Bob Burns joined the band, which changed its name to My Backyard. In 1968 they won a competition for up-and-coming bands and began to play the Florida club circuit. In 1970 the band changed its name once again, this time definitively: Ronnie Van Zant opted for Leonard Skinner (the spelling of which was changed to Lynyrd Skynyrd two years later). It was a tongue-in-cheek homage to his high school physical education teacher who had made a point of

punishing boys in the school who had long, "hippy-style" hair. Lynyrd Skynyrd (the other members besides Van Zant, Collins, Rossington and Burns, were Billy Powell, Leon Wilkeson and Ed King) began a long life on the road and in 1972 they were discovered, at an Atlanta concert, by the producer Al Kooper, who got them a contract with MCA Records where they recorded their first album, *Pronounced 'Leh-nérd 'Skin-hérd*. That album carried a song dedicated to one of the late heroes of Southern Rock, Duane Allman. The song's title was *Free Bird*, which went to number one in the American charts, a song that sounded like a sad presentiment. A year later Lynyrd Skynyrd opened The Who's show during their *Quadrophenia* tour and in 1974 released *Second Helping*, which was their biggest selling album. That album opened with a song that Van Zant wrote as a kind of response to two songs written by Neil Young, *Southern Man* and *Alabama*, which were very critical of southern racism. Young related how he had been attacked, in an Alabama bar, by a group of rednecks because of his hippy appearance, and Van Zant came back with *Sweet Home Alabama*. Thanks to its three-guitar attack, that song became one of the most

famous rock anthems, going to number 12 in the charts and ending up earning its parent album, *Second Coming*, a platinum certification. Lynyrd Skynyrd became an institution, conquering the public with their image as outlaws, and Ronnie Van Zant realised his dream of becoming the leading rock star in Jacksonville.

Describing the signature sound of his band, Ronnie once said: "We like to call ours 'Southern Raunchy Roll'. The other bands are just as bad, but we go to jail more." However, the following years were anything but easy: the albums *Nuthin' Fancy* and *Gimme Back My Bullets* did not achieve the same success and Bob Burns and Ed King left the band, which, in the meantime, had added drummer Artimus Pyle and three backup singers, Leslie Hawkins, JoJo Billingsley and Cassie Gaines. Ronnie Van Zant understood that Lynyrd Skynyrd had to regain the sound that had launched *Sweet Home Alabama* and, consequently, went in search of a new guitarist. The solution came courtesy of Cassie Gaines, who recommended her younger brother Steve, a blues virtuoso. The band asked Steve Gaines to sit in with them on 11 May 1976 during a show in Kansas City; he was asked to join

89 Ronnie Van Zant on stage with Lynyrd Skynyrd at Knebworth in 1976. "We like to call our music 'Southern Raunch Roll'," he stated. "The other bands are just as bad, but we go to jail more."

them the following month and took part in the studio recording of *Street Survivors*. That had been the springboard for a new talent who Van Zant himself said would soon overshadow the rest of the band. But that was to be his first and only album with Lynyrd Skynyrd. The cover photo of *Street Survivors* showed Lynyrd Skynyrd enveloped by flames and Steve with his eyes closed. A few months before the album was released Gary Rossington, who had been drunk and stoned, had had a bad car accident. Bad times were looming for the band.

Three days after *Street Survivors* was released, 20 October 1977, Lynyrd Skynyrd played in the Memorial Auditorium at Greenville, South Carolina. They had recently embarked on a tour, which had been going extremely well. They were to give a concert in Baton Rouge, Louisiana for which 10,000 tickets had already been sold. In order to have as many engagements as possible and to move about more rapidly, the band and its crew, 28 people in all, travelled in a Convair CV 300 airplane. That day, pilots Walter McCreary and William Gray took off at about 7.00 am. The musicians were celebrating their successful concert and some were playing poker. But the plane was low on fuel. The pilots reported their predicament to the control tower at McComb, Mississippi, which advised them to reverse course and make an emergency landing as visibility was very poor at McComb. The plane passed over the airport and tried to land in a clearing near Gillsburg, Mississippi. The crash was terrible. Johnny Mote, a farmer who lived nearby, said that he had heard a tremendous noise, as if the plane had been swallowed by the earth. The accident took the lives of both pilots, road manager Dean Kilpatrick, Cassie Gaines, Steve Gaines and Ronnie Van Zant. Artimus Pyle managed to crawl out of the plane and call for help. Many of the other passengers were seriously injured: Leon Wilkeson had broken his leg and his arm, Allen Collins suffered spinal trauma, Gary Rossington had multiple fractures to his legs and arms. Ronnie Van Zant's journey ended in a swamp in Mississippi, in the Deep South of the United States from where it had started. And Cassie Gaines and Steve Gaines's journey had only just begun.

90 and 91 Steve Gaines's first concert with Lynyrd Skynyrd was in Kansas City on 11 May 1976. It was his sister, Cassie Gaines, the band's chorus singer, who recommended him to the band. The following year both were in the terrible airplane crash that killed six persons and injured 20 others, as the headline of the *Enterprise Journal* reported the following day.

"GILLSBURG PLANE CRASH KILLS SIX, HURTS 20 INCLUDING ROCK SINGERS"

[Enterprise Journal]

KEITH MOON

[23 August 1946 > 7 September 1978]

They say that all rock drummers are crazy. But no one was as crazy as Keith Moon. "I'm still the best Keith Moon-style drummer in the world," he said of himself. He was an eccentric, a screwball, a self-destructive talent and a symbol of the transgressive rock 'n' roll lifestyle. And also a drummer prey to the delirium of the music he played. Keith Moon was the soul of The Who, just as Pete Townshend was the brain, Roger Daltrey the heart and John Entwistle the rhythm. In 1977 he said that he had gone adrift like a shipwreck without knowing where he was headed, without any aim, adding that he had to try to be a bit more disciplined. The following year Keith Moon died aged only 32, leaving behind a legendary series of rock 'n' roll anecdotes.

His musical career began in the Sea Cadet Corps band in London. Keith had played the bugle, but had changed to the drums after seeing the movie *Drum Crazy*, the story of jazz drummer Gene Krupa. By carefully observing such virtuosi as Gene Krupa, Jo Jones and Buddy Rich, Keith Moon developed the frenzied style and over-the-top behaviour that made him famous. In 1961 he bought his first drum kit and began to haunt the Music Club of the Oldfield Hotel, where he met the person who was his first and only teacher, Carlo Little, the drummer of the Savages, with whom he took lessons for a few weeks. In 1962 he joined his first band, The Escorts, and then played for a year with the Beachcombers, a band that specialised mostly in surf music and songs by Cliff Richard. His fellow band members remember him as a marriage of genius and lunacy. Keith Moon developed a passion for surf music and collected Dick Dale records, but his drum style was so uninhibited and frenetic that it soon passed well beyond the confines of surf music. In fact, he was too good for the Beachcombers who, in the meantime, had managed to record an album for the Columbia label, an instrumental piece called *Mad Goose*. In 1963, while he was working at odd jobs, including being an apprentice electrician and a stucco salesman for the British Gypsum company, Moon discovered that The Who no longer had a drummer, as Doug Sandom, who had played with them since they had been called The Detours, had been fired. Keith had already heard of their behaviour during their live sets, so he went to the Oldfield Hotel pub, in Greenford, dressed completely in orange. The Who were rehearsing with a session drummer. Keith said: "I can play better than him," sat at the drums and played Bo Diddley's *Road Runner* so hard that he smashed part of the drum kit, including the pedal of the bass drum and two drumheads. Keith later related that he was sitting at the bar, afterwards, when Roger asked him what he was doing that Monday. He replied that he sold stucco during the day but was free in the evening and Roger said he would have to leave that job because they had a show. "Nobody asked me join the group, they only asked me what I was doing on Monday." He was only 17.

From that time on, Keith Moon played on eight Who albums, from *My Generation* (1965) to *Who Are You* (1978), and he wrote the history of rock. But above all, he wrote an authentic manual of rock star madness. His specialty was destroying hotel toilets, as well those in his friends' houses, with thunderflash, cherry bombs and even dynamite. This was a real passion that resulted in his being banned for life from staying at many hotel chains in the United States, including the Holiday Inn, Sheraton and Hilton. His personal assistant Dougal Butler relates in Moon's biography *Full Moon*: "He would do anything if he knew that there were enough people around who didn't want him to do it." On the day of his 21st birthday Keith organized a party at the Holiday Inn in Flint, Michigan, and after blowing up the toilet in his room with dynamite he drove an automobile into the hotel swimming pool, breaking one of his teeth. On 4 January 1970, after triggering a row at the Red Lion Pub in Hatfield, he got into his Bentley while completely drunk and hit his chauffeur Neil Boland, killing him. On 20 November 1973, during the band's *Quadrophenia* tour, The Who held a concert in Daly City, near San Francisco, and Moon consumed a goodly amount of horse tranquilizers and brandy and fainted while he was playing *Won't Get Fooled Again*. An injection of cortisone put him right, but while playing *Magic Bus* he passed out again and had to be taken away. Pete Townshend then asked the audience: "Can anyone play the drums? I mean somebody good."

Many doctors who visited him to help him overcome his alcohol abuse declared that Keith was beyond hope. When his good friend Ringo Starr warned him that if he continued to act like this he would not live long, Keith merely replied: "Yeah, I know." From 1976 onwards his problems became ungovernable and the rock 'n' roll "loon" was taken away from the studio by his fellow band members while they were recording the vocal parts because he made them laugh so much they couldn't continue. His wife Kim Kerrigan divorced him in 1975 for mistreatment and prior to that had left him and taken their daughter Amanda to live with Faces keyboardist, Ian McLagan. The Who took a pause after their American tour, which ended on

21 October at the Maple Leaf Gardens in Toronto. Keith Moon was living in Malibu with his new girlfriend, Swedish model Annette Walter-Lax, but his lifestyle in California soon proved to be dangerous: he spent all his money on alcohol and drugs, passed entire days hanging out with Ringo Starr and Harry Nilsson, became bored and, therefore, got into trouble. Annette persuaded him to enter rehabilitation a number of times but without success. Each time he came out, Keith would start drinking again. In 1978 the situation seemed to be improving: The Who had bought a movie studio at Shepperton and were about to begin shooting a biographical film titled *The Kids Are Alright* and to record a new album, *Who Are You.*

94 top and bottom It has been estimated that the damage caused by Keith Moon's madcap behaviour during his 14-year career in rock 'n' roll amounted to about 500,000 dollars. The 8 September 1978 issue of the *Daily Mirror* underscores his tumultuous life and excesses in the article announcing his death.

94-95 The Who photographed for *Vogue* in 1969. From left to right, John Entwistle, Roger Daltrey, Pete Townshend and Keith Moon.

Keith returned to London and was happy to leave California and resume work. *Who Are You* would be his final album: in the cover photograph he is wearing one of his favourite costumes, that of a jockey, and is seated on a chair bearing a sentence that sounds like a macabre presentiment: "Not to be taken away." At first, Keith and Annette lived at the Kensington Palace Hotel, then they settled in an apartment, in Curzon Street, owned by Harry Nilsson, the same one where Mama Cass of the Mamas & Papas had died four years earlier.

The last years of Moon's life were a race to the grave. He was unable to play without his brandy and cocaine; he consumed large quantities of Valium and other medicines to combat his alcoholism. He vacationed in Mauritius but returned escorted by the police because he had gone into a rage on the plane that was taking him back home. A physician prescribed a cure with a sedative called Heminevrin and left him a bottle with 100 pills – a terrible mistake. On the evening of 6 September 1978, Keith and Annette attended a dinner organized by Paul

McCartney, on the anniversary of Buddy Holly's death, at the Peppermint Park restaurant, where they sat at the same table with McCartney, and afterwards went to the Dominion Theatre in Leicester Square to see the preview of the film *The Buddy Holly Story*. Keith and Annette left before the end. Keith wanted to see another movie, *The Abominable Dr. Phibes* directed by Robert Fuest. By then it was 7.00 am and he was hungry. He asked Annette to make him a steak with eggs. After this absurd breakfast he swallowed a handful of pills and went to sleep. At 4.00 pm Annette tried to wake him, but Keith had stopped breathing. She desperately phoned his personal doctor, Geoffrey Dymond, who could do nothing but verify his death. Moon had swallowed 32 Heminevrin pills.

The loudest and most exaggerated drummer in the history of rock had died in his sleep, in silence. Had he been able to choose, he would most certainly have concocted a more spectacular death. Perhaps he would have decided to fly into the air while blowing up the toilet in Harry Nilsson's cursed apartment.

"DRUGS DEATH DRAMA OF POP WILD MAN MOON"

[Daily Mirror]

96 Keith Moon on stage in 1975. The drummer was known for his wild, nonconformist temperament, which is discussed in the *Daily Mirror* article that lamented his dramatic death due to drug abuse.

97 The Who live in 1975: on stage are John Entwistle, Keith Moon and Pete Townshend.

SID
VICIOUS

99 Sid Vicious during the Sex Pistols' 1978 tour of America. "I'll die before I'm 25, and when I do I'll have lived the way I wanted to."

[10 May 1957 > 2 February 1979]

John Simon Ritchie was the biggest fan of the Sex Pistols. He was 20 years old at the time and spent all his time in the King's Road, in Malcolm McLaren and Vivienne Westwood's shop, "Sex," the starting point of the British punk revolution. He was supposedly the person who invented the violent dance that the public did during the band's concerts, the pogo. John was born in Lewisham, in Southeast London, to a family with problems. His mother was a junkie and his father a guardsman at Buckingham Palace who also played semi-professional trombone in London jazz clubs and who disappeared shortly after the boy's birth. In 1965 his mother remarried, Christopher Beverley, who died of cancer six months later. And John grew up on the streets, which were becoming the home of the punk lifestyle, an angry reaction of the younger generation to the rules of a society from which it felt excluded.

With the stage name Sid Vicious, he was a combination of everything punk rock represented: anarchy, violence, nihilism, excess and an arrogant indifference towards everything and everyone. He was destined for self-destruction from the very beginning. And it began when he met John Lydon, with whom he squatted in London houses together with John Wardle (alias Jah Wobble) and John Gray, a band that their friends called "The Four Johns." John Lydon also gave him his nickname: when his hamster Sid bit him on the leg he reacted by saying: "Sid is really vicious," so he became Sid Vicious. Malcolm McLaren said of him: "If Johnny Rotten is the voice of punk, Sid Vicious is the attitude."

The story of the Sex Pistols began in 1977 when the band asked Sid to replace bassist Glen Matlock. Earlier he had played in the Flowers of Romance, formed by Keith Levene of the Clash, and had played drums with Siouxsie & The Banshees during their first date at the 100 Club on Oxford Street. He didn't play the bass guitar well but had the right image for punk rock. For that matter, he was part of the Bromley Contingent, a group of Sex Pistols fans who helped to spread the punk fashion. And he had already acquired a bad reputation: he attacked a journalist with a rusty chain and was arrested at a Damned concert for having thrown a bottle into the audience, seriously injuring a girl. So he was perfect for launching the band to success and made his debut with them on 4 April 1977.

But his tragedy began immediately, with an encounter that proved to be fatal: that same year Johnny Thunders' band, The Heartbreakers, arrived in England, bringing with it a dangerous passion for heroin and a groupie, Nancy Spungen, who was a junkie. According to legend, it was Thunders who pushed a syringe under Sid's nose and taunted him: "Are you man or a boy?" Besides drugs, Sid was yoked to Nancy Spungen, who became his doomed soul mate. He was a rebel without a future and she had virtually grown up in a psychiatric clinic and, from the age of 15, had prostituted herself to pay for her heroin. In New York the people on the punk scene called her Nauseating Nancy. Sid and Nancy met, fell in love, and immediately isolated themselves in a dangerous world totally removed from reality. During the recording sessions for the Sex Pistols' first album, *Never Mind the Bollocks*, Sid was in no condition to play and the band had to ask Glen Matlock to return.

Everyone tried to persuade Sid to stay away from Nancy, in vain. The only moment they were separated was during the band's 1978 American tour, a crescendo of mad acts that led the band to break up after their last date at the Winterland Ballroom in San Francisco. Americans had never seen Sid Vicious in action and he did his very best to create an atmosphere of total chaos: in San Antonio he insulted the spectators by calling them a "group of queers," while in Dallas he went on stage showing the phrase "Gimme a Fix" on his chest that he had cut beforehand with razor blades.

Two days after the band's final concert, on 16 January 1978, he had a heroin overdose for the first time, and three days later fell into a coma during a flight to New York, once again due to drugs. When he returned to Europe, Sid took part in the shooting of the film *The Great Rock 'n' Roll Swindle* and recorded what proved to be his best contribution to the history of the band, a devastating and beautiful rendition of Frank Sinatra's *My Way*. The Sex Pistols broke

up, Johnny Rotten left his friend to his tragic destiny simply because he didn't know what to do to save him. In August 1978, Sid flew to New York to be with Nancy. They lived in room 100 of the Chelsea Hotel, the rock star hotel on 23rd Street. Sid formed a band, the Idols, that also included Jerry Nolan and Arthur Kane of the New York Dolls and he launched his new solo career with a series of dates at Max's Kansas City. Nancy was the band's manager and Malcolm McLaren financed them. The result was disastrous, partly because Sid was always too high to play.

He spent the rest of his life – marked by heroin and violence – in the Chelsea Hotel. And it ended in mystery. On the morning of 12 October 1978, Nancy Spungen was found in their room by a hotel employee; she was lying in a pool of blood with her abdomen slit open. Next to her was a knife, which was a gift from Sid. He was wandering in the hotel hallways, repeatedly muttering one word:

"Baby." What had happened that night? Nancy Spungen's death became a mystery. Sid's statements were contradictory. First he accused himself of the murder, which supposedly occurred after a row with Nancy, under the influence of drugs; then he said he had fallen asleep and found her dead when he woke up. The police did not make an investigation, since this case was too easy to close, and anyway one more dead junkie didn't interest anyone. Sid Vicious was arrested and put in Rikers Island prison, but was released, soon after, on 50,000 dollars bail put up by Virgin Records. He then entered Bellevue Hospital after attempting suicide. According to all those who knew him, Sid would never have killed Nancy. Too many pushers had gone to room 100 that night and Nancy had a suitcase filled with money. Malcolm McLaren engaged a team of detectives to find out whether Nancy had been murdered. Steve Dior, the guitarist of the Idols, blamed a New Jersey pusher. Suspicions were also cast

100 9 January 1978: the Sex Pistols during their first and only American tour at the Kingfisher Club in Baton Rouge, Louisiana: Sid Vicious, Johnny Rotten and Steve Jones.

101 Sid Vicious and Nancy Spungen. The two met in London in 1976. Their tormented relationship lasted 23 months and became known as one of the most tragic events in the history of rock 'n' roll. The day after Vicious died *The Sun* wrote that drugs had killed the punk star.

"DRUGS KILL PUNK STAR SID VICIOUS"

[The Sun]

on Rockets Redglare, a comic actor who provided the couple with psychotropic drugs. The truth never emerged and the case was closed.

At this point Sid Vicious' life fell apart. On 1 February 1979, he left the rehab clinic. His new girlfriend Michele Robinson organised a small welcome home party in their apartment at 63 Bank Street. Sid had already attempted to commit suicide three times. But now, at least, he was clean of drugs. Unfortunately, he was surrounded by drug addicts. A party was held to celebrate his being released on bail, and his mother, who arrived from London to see him, decided to buy some heroin. The pusher was a certain Peter Kodlick, who had pure heroin, which is always too strong for anyone who has just come out of a detox program. Sid collapsed, but Michele managed to revive him. He took another dose of his mother's heroin. At 3.00 am Michele put him to bed. The following morning Sid was found dead. He was only 21. Some say he committed suicide to be with Nancy again.

Many people think Sid Vicious was the true symbol of the punk spirit. Others consider him merely a tragic figure, a boy who was too weak and who became too famous.

BON SCOTT

The Highway to Hell is the nickname of the Canning Highway, an asphalt strip that runs through Australia and connects Freemantle to Perth. Bon Scott took that road many times to go to the Raffles Hotel, a rock 'n' roll bar in Applecross, in the suburbs of Perth, precisely at the Canning Highway-Canning Beach Road intersection. That was his favourite haunt, the place where he took part in legendary drinking bouts before continuing his journey down the *Highway to Hell*: "Hey, Momma, look at me, I'm on my way to the promised land, I'm on the highway to hell." Bon Scott was the lead singer of AC/DC, one of the most unconventional and noisiest rock bands of the 1970s. Like brothers Angus and Malcolm Young , he was born in Scotland and moved to Australia with his family. When he joined AC/DC he was already 27 and had a hair-raising past.

When still a boy he had ended up in a reformatory, the Riverbank Juvenile Institution (among other things, he was accused of having stolen twelve gallons of gasoline); he tried to enlist in the army but was rejected because he was considered "socially maladjusted"; he was one of the first musicians in Australia to have been arrested for drug possession (in 1970, while he was with his first band, The Valentines). Furthermore, he had just been released from hospital after a terrible motorcycle accident. On 3 May 1974, at the Old Lion Hotel in Adelaide, he had had a huge row with the members of his new band, the Mount Lofty Rangers, got onto his Suzuki 550, while completely drunk and in a rage, and had had a violent collision. He had been in a coma for three days and spent two weeks in hospital. When he was released, in order to make a living he had worked as a roadie

in the booking agency of a friend, Vince Lovegrove, who promoted promising bands. Bon was a first-rate blues and rock 'n' roll performer, but he had never been able to stop drinking and getting into trouble. One day he heard that AC/DC was looking for a new singer. The Angus Young-Bon Scott combination proved to be an explosive cocktail: while the youngster Angus was bad news, Bon was the personification of the devil of rock. Bon's voice – a hysterical falsetto that grated like sandpaper, consisting of blues, cigarettes and bottles of whisky – was precisely the element that the AC/DC sound had been lacking, and when their lead singer Dave Evans did not show up for a gig, Bon Scott replaced him. "My grandfather had a bakery and I worked with him," Scott said. "The only prospect I had was to bake bread instead of only kneading it. Rock 'n' roll saved me." With Bon Scott, AC/ DC wrote the history of hard rock, releasing one album a year – all the same, very fast, and launched in concerts that were more and more spectacular. Bon Scott was like a fortress in the middle of the stage: nude from the waist up, legs spread out and sporting a fiendish sneer. Angus Young would run around him dressed like a schoolboy, letting fly with lethal solos. The result was brutal rock that was so coarse it was unique.

High Voltage came out in 1974, followed by *TNT, Dirty Deeds Done Dirt Cheap* and *Let There Be Rock*, which opened the road to success in America as well. *Powerage* was released in 1978 and the following year the band launched its first million-seller, *Highway to Hell*, which was in the American Top 20 and achieved seventh in the British charts. The band was ready to conquer the world: "All groups have ups and downs," Angus Young once

said, "but with us everything is always the same. We have what all kids want. They want rock and we give it to them." Unfortunately, at the peak of success, Bon Scott made his exit in a most absurd manner.

On 19 February 1980, he was in his apartment at Ashley Court, in London. A friend, Alistair Kinnear, called him and asked him to go to a party at the Music Machine, a club in Camden Town, and then went to pick him up in his Renault 5. He drank quite a lot at the club, as did Kinnear. The situation was getting out of hand. While they were going back home in the car Bon Scott fell asleep and, when they arrived at Ashley Court, Alistair couldn't wake him up. He looked for the apartment keys and went in to ask Bon's girlfriend to help him but she was out. Alistair then decided to take Bon to his own house at Overhill Road in East Dulwich. Once again he tried to waken him and tried to carry him indoors but to no avail. Then he decided to do something totally inexplicable: he lowered Bon's seat, covered him with a blanket and left him in the car to sleep it off. It was the dead of night and it was cold. Alistair left a note with his address and phone number in case of need and then went to bed. He woke up the next afternoon and at 7.00 pm went to the car. Bon Scott was still there but he wasn't breathing. Alistair rushed him to King's College Hospital, but it was too late Bon Scott was already dead. The physicians wrote a chilling report: "Accidental death caused by alcohol poisoning." Ronald Belford Scott, who was born in Kirriemuir, Scotland, 33 years earlier, drank up until the last moment of his life. The highway to hell was a peaceful street in a residential neighbourhood of London.

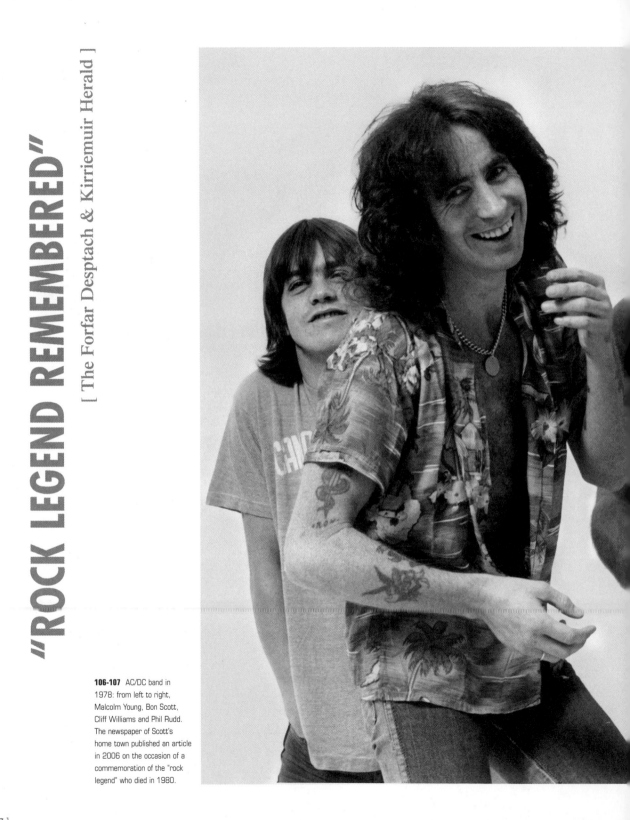

"ROCK LEGEND REMEMBERED"
[The Forfar Desptach & Kirriemuir Herald]

106-107 AC/DC band in 1978: from left to right, Malcolm Young, Bon Scott, Cliff Williams and Phil Rudd. The newspaper of Scott's home town published an article in 2006 on the occasion of a commemoration of the "rock legend" who died in 1980.

IAN
CURTIS

[15 July 1956 > 18 May 1980]

Macclesfield is a somewhat dull, uninviting town in Cheshire, in the industrial north of England, where Ian Curtis spent almost his entire life. He had been born in Manchester on 15 July 1956 and lived with his parents until 1973, in their apartment in Victoria Park, Macclesfield. He loved music and idolised David Bowie and Iggy Pop, and he worked in Rare Records, a Manchester record shop. Ian was born into a generation that had been struck by punk and that, through music, could express the anger and sense of solitude it had always felt so strongly. He was also an artist who, with his band Joy Division, would create a style that would influence British music for two decades. Joy Division enchanted the public with its rarefied music, desperate lyrics and the dreamy, introspective atmosphere that filled the void that had been left by punk and which critics began to associate with the word "dark." But Ian Curtis was, above all, one of the most tragic and sublime figures in the history of rock music, a boy from Macclesfield who decided to end his life when he was only 23.

His entire life had moved quickly: he had married, when only 19, to a school friend, Deborah Woodruffe. The couple moved into 77 Barton Street in Macclesfield, the same house in which Deborah found him dead on the morning of 16 May 1980. Ian had hanged himself with a washing line. His band, Joy Division, had been about to leave for a tour of the United States. What happened in Ian Curtis's life?

She's Lost Control and *Love Will Tear Us Apart* are the Joy Division songs that narrate Ian's descent into darkness. His career as a rock star began with an overwhelming awakening sparked by the Sex Pistols' second concert at the Lesser Free Trade Hall in Manchester, on 20 June 1976. About 100 people had been there, including Ian Curtis, Bernard Sumner, Peter Hook and a friend of theirs, Terry Mason. The following day Hook had asked his mother for a loan of 35 pounds and had bought a

bass guitar. Ian decided he wanted to become a rock singer, which he did by answering an ad that Sumner had put in a record store in Manchester stating that he was looking for a vocalist for the band he had formed with Peter Hook and Terry Mason. The name was Warsaw, from a song by David Bowie (*Warszawa*, on the album *Low*). They played their first gig on 19 May 1977 at the Electric Circus, opening for the Buzzcocks. In August 1977 drummer Stephen Morris joined the band, which became Joy Division, from a disturbing 1955 novel, *The House of Dolls*, which described how women were abused in the Joy Division, a section of a Nazi concentration camp. The band's transformation into the most influential band of the next three decades took place on New Year's Eve 1978 with their final concert as Warsaw, in Liverpool. In his house on Barton Street, Ian Curtis had filled dozens of notebooks with poems and songs. Rock had become the vehicle through which he could express himself and deal with his anxieties. And he had also found an extraordinary companion for his adventures, Tony Wilson. Wilson, a presenter, TV show host and journalist for Granada Television and the BBC, had also attended the Sex Pistols' performance at the Lesser Free Trade Hall. They met after a Joy Division gig at the Rafters Club in Manchester on 14 April: Ian had complained that his band had never been invited to appear on Wilson's *So It Goes* TV program and Wilson replied that they were next on the list. In June 1978 Joy Division released an EP on their label: *An Ideal For Living*. Two months later they appeared on *So It Goes*, presenting two songs (*Digital* and *Glass*) from their *A Factory Sample* compilation, the first official release by Factory Records, the label they co-founded with Wilson. The Factory Records and Joy Division collaboration marked the beginning of a career that became a symbol of the Manchester music scene as well as an example of the indie rock ethic for all future British music.

109 Joy Division was formed in Salford, Manchester, in 1976. Their recording debut was the EP *An Ideal for Living*, which they produced themselves in 1978.

But Ian soon discovered he was a doomed person: after a concert at the Hope and Anchor pub in London, he had an epileptic fit while the band was going back home in a car – epilepsy is an illness that certainly does not fit in with the reckless, excessive lifestyle of a rock star. Ian felt that he would not live long. There was one episode in particular that had upset him. During the early days of Joy Division, Ian was also active as a social worker, first in an employment agency in Manchester and then in a rehabilitation centre for the disabled in Macclesfield. Among his patient list, one day, was a woman who had suffered from epilepsy and had missed her appointment. *She's Lost Control*: the woman had died. Ian was terrorized. On stage he would mime the movements and twitches of an epileptic seizure in a macabre dance. Often the strobe lighting in clubs would trigger a seizure, but the audience never knew whether he was really suffering or was merely dancing. The doctors prescribed phenobarbitone, a medicine with powerful side effects. Ian fell into a deep depression, while in the meantime the world of Joy Division was exploding around him. In 1979 they recorded their first album, *Unknown Pleasures*, which was released with a legendary cover designed by Peter Saville. It sold 10,000 copies and, according to Tony Wilson (who had paid for the recording out of his own pocket), it transformed Factory Records into a revolutionary power that was able to subvert the entire British recording system from within. Those 10,000 copies would become a manifesto for a generation of bands that has adhered to that distorted and electronic rock sound to this day. Joy Division went on a UK tour consisting of 24 dates, to be followed by a brief European tour.

But Ian Curtis was ill. His seizures had become stronger and stronger. And his life went to pieces when in October 1979, after a concert in Brussels, he met journalist, Annik Honoré, who became his lover. *Love Will Tear Us Apart*: the marriage between the two youngsters from Macclesfield had been destroyed by that infidelity. Deborah wanted a divorce. But there had been a new album that had had to be recorded, *Closer,* and a tour of America that might be the road to success over there for Joy Division. There had been far too much pressure for such a fragile person. On 7 April 1980 he had made his first attempt at suicide using phenobarbitone, but had told Deborah, who had saved his life by taking him to hospital. The following day the band had been due to play at Derby Hall in Bury. Simon Topping, from A Certain Ratio, stood in for Ian for part of the show,

which led to strong protests, from some of the audience, that ended in a riot. Many engagements had had to be cancelled, yet Joy Division had managed to shoot a video for the single *Love Will Tear Us Apart,* and they played their final gig at Birmingham University on 2 May 1980. The last song Ian sang had been *Digital*. On 19 May the band had been scheduled to leave for its first American tour. Ian was not present. No one knows whether his suicide had been a sudden act of desperation or something planned well in advance. In her book, *Touching From a Distance,* Deborah wrote that, in her opinion, Ian had agreed to go on the tour not to please his fellow band members or Factory Records, but because he already knew he would never get on the airplane.

Their daughter Natalie, a photographer, and the other members of Joy Division maintain that the fault lay with the medication he took to combat his epilepsy, as it seemed to deprive him of his will to live. Ian knew he would never get well and that he would die soon, just like the woman from Macclesfield. What he had wanted most was to be with his wife Deborah and little Natalie, to become a rock star, to play music and to live a life that he felt he would never be allowed to live. So, in just a single night, he lost all hope. A tragic night, later related masterfully by photographer Anton Corbijn in his 2007 movie *Control*.

Ian Curtis had been alone in his house on Barton Street, where he hadn't actually resided for quite some time. In fact, he had been staying at his parents' home, having left the apartment to Deborah, who had been working nights as a waitress at a club. That evening he had just passed by to see her, and they had spoken about their love, their daughter and their forthcoming divorce, about which Deborah was resolute. She went to work and Ian watched *Stroszek*, a movie, directed by Werner Herzog, which tells the story of a suicide. When Deborah had returned home at dawn he had still been awake. She had offered to stay with him, but he had asked her to leave and not to come back until 10.00 am, when he would already have been on the train to Manchester. He stayed alone and listened to his final record, Iggy Pop's *The Idiot*. He had then written a long love letter to Deborah. Deborah returned, parked in front of the house, and left little Natalie to wait in the car. She found Ian in the kitchen, where he had hanged himself.

When he was a boy he had often said that he had wanted to live a short and intense life and that he would not live to be 25. Deborah had the title of his signature song carved on his tomb in Macclesfield: *Love Will Tear Us Apart.*

JOHN
BONHAM

[31 May 1948 > 25 September 1980]

113 John "Bonzo" Bonham in 1974. Robert Plant had the following to say about him: "John was the greatest drummer in the world. I knew this because he told me so."

He looked more like a beast than a man and, in fact, one of his nicknames was 'The Beast'. John "Bonzo" Bonham was the most powerful and exaggerated rock drummer and he played in a band that took the world by storm with its furious hard rock sound that someone called The Hammer of the Gods. The band was Led Zeppelin. Robert Plant, Jimmy Page, John Paul Jones and John Bonham acted like gods, embraced the rock 'n' roll lifestyle to the hilt and seemed to be indestructible. That was especially true of Bonham, who always played as if the world were crumbling around him. But in the end it was he who crumbled under the weight of a life of excess.

John Henry Bonham was born in Redditch, England in 1948. He never took a formal lesson. He hammered on anything at hand, from his mother's pots to a kind of drum his father made for him out of metal coffee tin. As a teenager he worked with his father in the latter's building business, while in the meantime playing in different local bands, including Terry Webb and the Spiders, The Nicky James Movement and The Senators. Then he joined Robert Plant's first band, Crawling King Snakes. John and Robert immediately became friends, and everyone called him "Bonzo," after the name of the kind and silent dog in a famous English animated cartoon. John idolised Ginger Baker of Cream and Keith Moon of The Who. He played with the same power and also began to line the inside of his drums with tin foil to imitate the explosive sound of a machine gun. Many clubs were not willing to engage him because he was too noisy. As a result, Bonham developed a softer sound and also learned to roll loudly without drumming so hard. Furthermore, he was one of the first drummers to play solos with his bare hands. When Robert Plant formed Band of Joy, Bonzo was his first choice as its drummer. The band secured dates in London clubs such as Speakeasy; they also opened for American singer Tim Rose during his UK tour. Plant and Bonham loved to play together, but Band of Joy soon broke up and Bonzo became the drummer in Tim Rose's band. Robert and John saw each other again at Oxford one evening in 1968. Robert had a lot to tell his friend: he had joined an extraordinary band, Jimmy Page's New Yardbirds. Bonzo was not enthusiastic at first, since he was earning 40 pounds a week with Tim Rose. But in July 1968, Jimmy Page heard Bonham play for the first time, at the Country Club in London and immediately knew how his new band should sound. Bonham's entry into the band was legendary. He didn't have a telephone, so Page literally bombarded him with telegrams – which he sent to John's favourite club, Three Men in a Boat, in Walsall – asking him to join the band. But Bonzo was still disinclined: he was also receiving offers from Joe Cocker and Joe Farlowe. "I thought the Yardbirds were finished, but I knew that Page was a fine guitarist and Plant was a friend, so in the end I thought it would be great to play in a good group."

So John Bonham became the New Yardbirds drummer. A bass guitarist, John Paul Jones, also joined the band. Jones later related how they met for the first time in a very small room to see if they could play together. They didn't even know what to play and finally agreed on *Train Kept A-Rollin*. Bonzo hit the drums and the room exploded: "As soon as I heard John play," Jones said, "I knew this was going to be great." On 14 September the band left for Copenhagen, beginning the Scandinavian tour that marked the birth of Led Zeppelin.

Between 1968 and 1979 the band recorded nine albums, from *Led Zeppelin* to *In Through the Out Door*, took America by storm with a series of sensational tours and became the greatest rock band in the world. Until the day when the driving force behind their sound, The Beast, John Bonham, passed away. The man who had given a new image to the excess and folly of rock stars died when he was only 32.

In April 1980 the band began to rehearse for a brief European promotional tour for *In Through the Out Door*, which ended with two dates at Knebworth Park in England to an audience of over 100,000. The original plan was to have 14 dates in June, in Germany, the Netherlands, Belgium and Switzerland, their first concerts in continental Europe since 1973. This time there were no new albums to promote and no exaggerated set, only the power and mystery of Led Zeppelin and their Hammer of the Gods sound. But the band had already fallen victim to their exaggerated lifestyle and drug abuse. Bonzo was getting fatter and fatter; he had stopped using heroin but was drinking a huge amount of alcohol. At the Melody Maker award ceremony he was completely drunk and, despite the fact that Led Zeppelin won hands down, he proclaimed Police to be the best band of the year, singing the refrain of *Message in a Bottle* at the top of his voice. During their Nuremberg concert on 27 June, he fainted after the third song. In Frankfurt a few days later he suddenly got up from the drum stand, during the execution of *White Summer*, and went to hug the president of Atlantic Records, Ahmet Ertegun. The tour ended in Berlin on 7 July 1980. Two months later the band got together again, to rehearse for their forthcoming American tour, at the Old Mill

House, Jimmy Page's home in Clewer. The band was ready to show that they were still the best in the world: Jimmy Page stated, in an interview, that he had had the sensation there was still a lot to give and that the band's existence was based on a continuous wager. But the story of Led Zeppelin ended with its drummer's last night of excess.

On 24 September 1980 the band's assistant, Rex King, went to pick up Bonham at his country house, the Old Hyde Farm. Bonzo wanted to stop off at a pub before going to the rehearsal. He was taking Motival, a tranquiliser, to relieve his anxiety attacks, but continued to drink. At the pub, he had his own version of breakfast: two ham sandwiches and four quadruple shots of vodka and orange juice. He resumed drinking at the studio until he was no longer able to play. This was truly unique, because, in twelve years, he had never missed a Led Zeppelin concert or rehearsal. But this time he didn't make it. The band then went to the Old Mill House for a small party. Bonham drank two or three more double vodkas and went to sleep on a sofa. Jimmy Page's assistant, Rick Hobbs, was accustomed to such scenes and dragged Bonzo to a bedroom, placed him on his side with his head on some pillows. The band waited for the Beast to sober up for the umpteenth time. But this did not happen. At 2.00 pm another assistant, Benji LeFevre, found him dead in the bedroom. He was still lying on his side, but the precautions Hobbs had taken proved to be futile: John Bonham had died by choking on his own vomit. How could this be? The only explanation was the huge quantity of alcohol he had consumed, which would have destroyed anyone. But many people, especially the press, did not believe that. There had always been an aura of mystery and doom surrounding Led Zeppelin and the death of John Bonham was the latest proof of it. Jimmy Page was an occultist and also collected objects that had once belonged to Aleister Crowley, a famous occultist and mystic. Page also bought a villa at Loch Ness in Scotland. A fanzine wrote that the day John died, thick black smoke emerged from Page's house. The London *Evening News* published an article asserting that Bonham had died because of the black magic practised by Page. The police searched Page's villa but found nothing suspicious there. A physician stated that Bonham's death was caused by an accidental overdose of alcohol.

John Bonham was buried in Rushock, a short distance from his farm. He left a wife Pat and two children Jason and Zoe. Was it a question of fatality or fate? Led Zeppelin felt they could not go on playing without Bonzo and, on 4 December 1980, issued a press statement announcing they were disbanding: "We wish it to be known that the loss of our dear friend, and the deep sense of undivided harmony felt by ourselves and our manager, have led us to decide that we could not continue as we were."

ROCK GROUP'S FEARS AFTER TRAIL OF TRAGEDY

'Black magic vengeance killed Zeppelin star'

BONHAM . . . mystery death.

THE death of Led
Zeppelin drummer John

By JOHN BLAKE

" It sounds crazy, but Robert
Plant and everyone around

114 John Bonham during Led Zeppelin's tour of America in 1978. Bonham stated: "I really like to yell out when I'm playing. I yell like a bear to give it a boost. I like our act to be like a thunderstorm."

115 top 17 May 1975: Led Zeppelin performing at Earl's Court in London: Robert Plant, Jimmy Page, John Paul Jones and John Bonham.

115 bottom The headline of the *Evening News* that accuses Jimmy Page and his passion for black magic and occultism of having caused Bonzo's death.

DARBY CRASH

[26 September 1958 > 7 December 1980]

A suicide pact: that was the sad story of Darby Crash. The malaise of young white Americans that turns into tragedy – with the aid of heroin. On 7 December 1980 Jan Paul Beahm was only 22 but was convinced that he had no future. His life had been a disaster. He had grown up with an alcoholic mother, had thought that his father had abandoned him and discovered later that his real father had been a Swedish sailor. He had changed his name, first to Bobby Pyn and then to Darby Crash, in search of an identity. And then he had found punk rock and, finally, heroin, which became his great passion. However, in the meantime Darby had managed to become a legend on the Los Angeles punk scene, thanks to the band he had formed in 1977, with his friend Georg Ruthenberg (known as Pat Smear), The Germs. It was a chaotic, noisy band, totally out of control. Their concerts were explosions of madness and violent: Darby Crash sang everywhere except into the microphone, he wounded himself on stage, like his idol Iggy Pop, and he roused the audience to fever pitch. And there had been an endless flow of alcohol and heroin. The Germs recorded only two singles, a demo and one official album, *(GI)* – which was produced by Joan Jett of The Runaways and was released in 1979 – but they had a great influence on all of the American indie rock of later years. Many people consider *(GI)* to have been the first hardcore album ever produced. But Darby Crash, when only 22 years old, no longer wanted to live. He said as much to Pat Smear and his other friends. On 3 December 1980 The Germs gave a concert at the Starwood Club in Los Angeles. They broke up and then re-formed again. Darby told his audience: "You won't be seeing us any more." Word had it that he had organized this concert only to scrape up enough money for his final overdose: 400 dollars worth of pure China White. The only person who knew what had been happening was his friend Casey Cola. They had made a suicide pact: they would die of a heroin overdose together. Darby shot up and then began to write a note – "Here lies Darby C..." – that he didn't manage to finish. He fell to the floor and died. Casey survived the overdose. California punk had found its ill-fated hero.

117 Jan Paul Beahm, known as Darby Crash, performing with the Darby Crash Band at the Starwood Club in Los Angeles on 3 December 1980. Four days later Darby died of a drug overdose. The headline in *The Observer* announced his death.

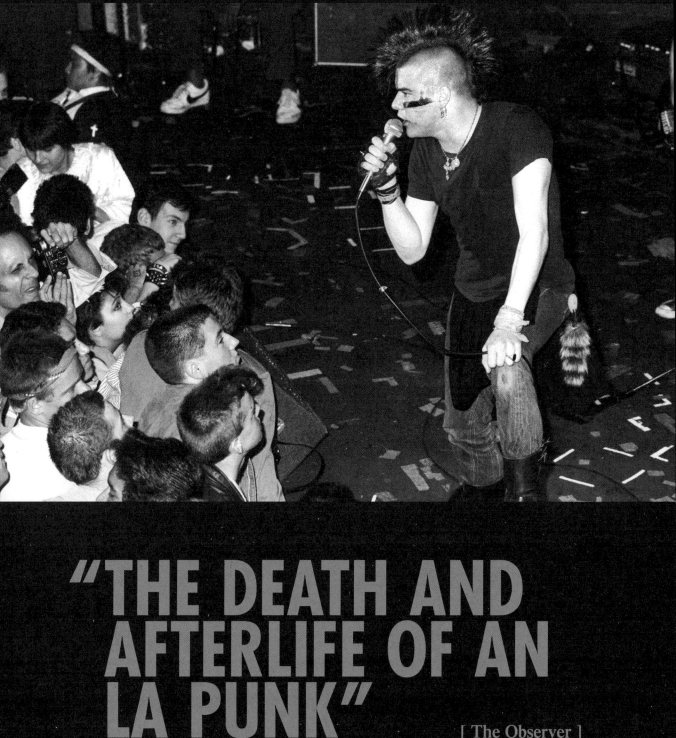

"THE DEATH AND AFTERLIFE OF AN LA PUNK"

[The Observer]

JOHN LENNON

New York, the city that never sleeps, that leaves you speechless and swallows you up in its frenetic vortex. New York, which may even kill you some time. Especially if you were born in Liverpool during the Second World War and have become a living legend, a guru worth a fortune, the critical conscience of the 20th century. John Lennon and the Big Apple had a strange relationship that suddenly ended during the evening of 8 December 1980 in front of the Dakota Building, in New York's Upper West Side, at the northwest corner of 71st Avenue and Central Park West. Mark David Chapman fired five shots, four of which hit their target. The former Beatle remained on the ground. Forever. He, who wanted to stay in Manhattan for a long time. His green card had finally arrived, after a long legal battle, and his family was united. John often said: "If I'd lived in Roman times, I'd have lived in Rome. Where else? Today America is the Roman Empire and New York is Rome itself."

His first New York address was 105 Bank Street, Greenwich Village, a stone's throw from the White Horse Tavern, a favourite haunt of Dylan Thomas and Jack Kerouac. That was during the time when Lennon was a solo artist and performed with Yoko Ono, the time of their "Bed-In for Peace" and other pacifist protests. In September 1971 Lennon released *Imagine*, the summer of 1972 saw the release of *Sometime in New York City* followed by *Mind Games* the following year. Artistic production and the city. He was crazy about New York and about Yoko yet he abandoned them both for "only" 18 months. He called that his "lost weekend" in Los Angeles (with a lot of debauchery and rock 'n' roll together with old and new friends, including Elton John). Then, John returned to Manhattan to devote all his time and energy to his wife, and son Sean who was born in 1975. He took five years "leave" from music, from the limelight and from mass media battles. Then he made a comeback; in October 1980 the single *(Just Like) Starting Over* was released,

followed a month later by the album *Double Fantasy*. In his last interview, which he gave during the morning of 8 December 1980, when he had just turned 40, John announced that he wanted to go back to working full-time, on his own, as he had always been, even when he played with the other Beatles and he and Paul had used the same microphone. Lennon was always one step ahead, had one more idea and it didn't matter whether it was wrong. John dreamed of peace and a world where people made love and not war, he believed in a world without Heaven or Hell and without religion. That last phrase was fatal. Mark David Chapman, a mentally disturbed 25 year-old, a Beatles fanatic and a fanatical Christian, planned to kill Lennon after hearing that and other statements from Lennon. He left Honolulu on 5 December and went to New York with the intention of killing him. He was convinced that Lennon had become an enemy, a rich bourgeoisie who had betrayed his ideals and lived in a luxurious apartment. Chapman wanted to become famous, like Lennon, by eliminating him for good. He waited outside from the early hours of the morning, carrying a copy of J.D. Salinger's famous novel *The Catcher in the Rye*. At 5.00 pm Lennon left the recording studio. Chapman asked him to autograph a copy of *Double Fantasy*. "Is that all?" Lennon asked. "Do you need something else?" The photographer Paul Goresh took a famous photograph of the victim and his assassin at that moment. "At that point I wanted to go back to my hotel," Chapman declared, "but I couldn't. I waited until he came back. He knew where the ducks went in winter and I needed to know this." That was a reference to Salinger's book, which he loved. He remained outside the building and waited for Lennon, in the darkness. At 10.49 pm John got out of his car in front of the Dakota Building. Chapman called out: "Mr. Lennon" and then shot him. John remained on the ground. His glasses and a tape with a demo of the song *Walking on Thin Ice* had fallen with him. "I want to see Sean before he goes to sleep," he had just said to Yoko Ono.

119 1964: John Lennon receiving letters from his fans. Beatlemania was the first example of mass fan hysteria in the history of rock music. The term appeared for the first time in the *Daily Mirror* on 2 November 1963.

120 25 March 1969: Five days after their wedding, John Lennon and Yoko Ono received journalists in their room (no. 702) at the Hilton Hotel in Amsterdam. This was the first "bed-in," a sort of artistic performance the couple engaged in to protest against the Vietnam War. John and Yoko stayed in their bed until 31 March.

120-121 The Beatles in 1964: Ringo Starr, Paul McCartney, John Lennon and George Harrison. Ringo joined the band in 1962 as a replacement for Pete Best.

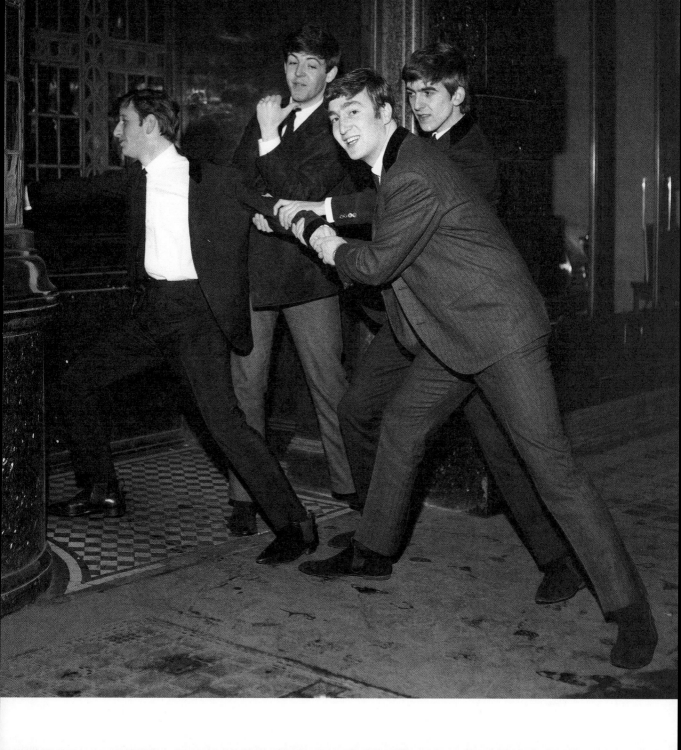

DAILY Mirror

SPECIAL ISSUE

Wednesday, December 10, 1980   12p   • • •

JOHN LENNON shot dead in New York Dec 8 1980 DEATH OF A HERO

SUPERSTAR: One of the last pictures of ex-Beatle John Lennon, taken in New York three weeks ago.

PLEASE TURN TO PAGES TWO and THREE

Daily Mail

WEDNESDAY, DECEMBER 10, 1980   12p

MONEY MAIL TODAY

Mail Picture Exclusive—The autograph that led to murder

LENNON AND HIS KILLER

IT'S 5 p.m. in New York. Amateur photographer Paul Goresh snaps a seemingly ordinary moment in the life of ex-Beatle John Lennon. Outside his home, the elegant Dakota apartment building, a stranger mumbles a request for an autograph, just like countless thousands before. A scribbled signature, and it's forgotten. But the smirking Mark Chapman was no ordinary fan. When Lennon returned to the same spot from a recording session, he was again waiting—with a gun. Chapman stepped from the shadows and callously and coolly gunned the singer down. It was 11 p.m. in New York...

INSIDE : Lennon Assassination 2, 3, 23, 24, 25, 26, World Weather 2, Lynda Lee-Potter 7, Diary 17, TV Guide 32, 33, Prize Crossword 39, Classified 42, 43

124 and 124-125 On 14 December 1980, millions of people throughout the world reacted positively to Yoko Ono's appeal for ten minutes silence in memory of John Lennon. In New York City, over 200,000 fans gathered in Central Park, in front of the Dakota Building. At least two Beatles fans committed suicide after Lennon's death, forcing Yoko to make an appeal in the *Daily News* discouraging such rash acts.

126-127 The John Lennon Museum in Saitama, Japan, which was inaugurated on 9 October 2000, on what would have been Lennon's 60th birthday, and closed on 30 September 2010. "Life is what happens while you are making other plans," Lennon once said.

BOB MARLEY

"Me got no education, me got inspiration. If I was educated I'd be a damn fool." Bob Marley had been the first Third World super star, an artist who led the traditional music of his land, Jamaica, to worldwide success. He became an idol for his people and for the world public, for that matter, who identified with his messages of peace and tolerance, as well as with his protest anthems against the injustice of modern society. And his adventurous life acquired all the characteristics of legend: Tuff Gong, the warrior musician, the prophet of the Rastafari religion, the poet of a just world. That life ended on 11 May 1981, when he was only 36 years old.

Robert Nesta Marley had been born in the village of Nine Mile, to a Jamaican woman, Cedella Booker, and a white British Naval officer, Norval Sinclair Marley. He used to relate that he had been born in Babylon, with a history of slaves, and that white men exploited black people. At the age of 12 Bob moved to 56 Hope Road in the Trench Town ghetto of Kingston, the centre of the largest Rastafari community in Jamaica. He had lived on the streets among the *sufferah*, young gang members. He listened to rhythm & blues, went to the contests among the sound systems of the first rock steady DJs and, instinctively, found his means of expression in music. He began to sing with a guitar which had a sardine tin for a body and telephone wires for strings, seated under a tree in front of his house in Hope Road, with his buddy

Neville "Bunny" Livingston. He recorded his first single, *Judge Not*, in 1962, for producer Leslie Kong's Beverley's label, and during a jam session with the musician Joe Higgs he met another bellicose musician, Peter McIntosh (later known as Peter Tosh). In 1963 Bob, Peter Tosh, Bunny Livingstone (alias Bunny Wailer), Junior Braithwaite, Beverley Kelso and Cherry Smith founded a band called The Teenagers, whose name was changed to The Wailers because, as the band members later stated, they came from the ghetto, where poor people wail because no one helps them, and they were the only persons who expressed the feelings of those people. The Wailers recorded one of their first protest songs, *Simmer Down*, signed a contract with Coxsone Dodd's Studio One label and began to become known in Jamaica. In 1966 Marley married Rita Anderson and decided to live near his mother in the United States, where he worked in a Chrysler factory in Wilmington, Delaware. When he returned to Jamaica he decided to devote his life to reggae. He worked with the producer Lee Scratch Perry and then met Chris Blackwell, the founder of Island Records. Blackwell knew that The Wailers could change the music scene, and Marley had begun to create a new type of reggae that was more varied and had an international flavour; he incorporated elements of blues and rock and, as the basis of the music, he replaced the heavy bass and drum rhythm with that of the guitar and the melody.

In 1972, in the UK, Island Records released The Wailers' first album, *Catch a Fire*, followed by *Burnin'* (1973). A year later, following two hugely successful American tours, Bob Marley had become a benchmark. Eric Clapton was the first person to recognize the importance of the reggae revolution created by Marley and recorded his cover of *I Shot the Sheriff*. Peter Tosh and Bunny Wailer left the band and in 1974 Marley released *Natty Dread*, which, thanks to the track *No Woman No Cry*, reached the top ten in the American charts. 1976 saw the success of *Rastaman Vibration*, an album of pure reggae mysticism that contained one of his most inspired songs, *War*.

Marley had become an international star and, in Jamaica, was considered to be a Rasta prophet and was considered to be a threat by the white Establishment. On 3 December 1976 he was wounded during an assault on his home by unknown gunmen. He then spent two years of self-imposed exile in London, where he recorded *Exodus* (1977), his most powerful and complete album, on which he passed from the reggae of *Jammin'* to the biblical mysticism of *Exodus*: "We know where we're going, uh! / We know where we're from. / We're leaving Babylon, / We're going to our Fatherland." The year 1978 witnessed the release of *Kaya*, an album entirely dedicated to marijuana and its mystical and spiritual qualities. In the meantime Marley and The Wailers continued to take their reggae show to an international audience

129 Bob Marley photographed in Jamaica in 1979. He stated that reggae would become a form of struggle if it hadn't already done so. According to him reggae was the music of the Third World and he said that you shouldn't try to understand it in one day but absorb it a little at a time and let it grow inside you.

with a series of tours in Europe and America whose atmosphere was best epitomised in the live album *Babylon By Bus* (1978). The following year Marley returned to Jamaica for a reconciliation concert, since his country was on the verge of civil war. He was greeted by the people as a prophet and, during *Jammin'*, at the One Love Peace Concert, he managed to get the leaders of the two rival factions, Michael Manley and Edward Seaga, to shake hands. At the end of 1978 he visited Ethiopia for the first time and then returned to the recording studio and released *Survival* (1979), a very politically orientated album recorded as an exhortation to combat oppression throughout the world. In 1980 Marley returned to Africa to play some live concerts to those he considered his people. After the initial concert in Gabon, he had been invited to play on the occasion of the proclamation of independence of Zimbabwe. A few months later the album *Uprising* was released, and during the Tuff Gong Uprising Tour in 1980 he also went to Italy for a historic concert at San Siro stadium in Milan. But his legend was about to end.

Bob Marley's legacy to the world had been his interpretation of reggae and a universal message: "I do not have the answers. I'm just a man. I know some words and know how to use them." But how does a prophet die? By following his passions. And Marley had three passions: music, women and football. He had 11 children by eight different women, including Cindy Breakspeare, the 1978 Miss Universe, the woman who inspired *Turn Your Lights Down Low*. He loved women and football. A month after *Exodus* had been released, Bob and The Wailers had begun a tour of Europe, in Paris. While playing football with a group of journalists had he injured his right foot and the nail of his big toe had fallen off (the same toe had already been injured in 1975, while he was playing in Trench Town). Bob bandaged the toe but did not have an anti-tetanus injection. The wound did not heal and his daughter Cedella had to medicate it every day. A French physician suggested a period of absolute rest, but Bob continued the tour and also went on playing football whenever he could. In London he was visited by a specialist, who advised him to have the toe amputated. Bob refused, because according to his religion one's body should remain whole. The untended wound became a tumour that gradually spread to his vital organs. He was given only a few months to live. He went to Miami and then Germany, to the clinic of the famous oncologist Josef Issels, and eventually returned to Jamaica. During the flight his condition worsened. When the plane landed at Miami he was immediately taken to the Cedars of Lebanon hospital, where he died on 11 May 1981. A state funeral was held for him in Jamaica and his tomb at Nine Mile became a pilgrimage site for Rastafarians. But Bob Marley's farewell had been made on stage during the sound check for his final concert on 23 September 1980 at the Stanley Theater in Pittsburgh. Marley had gathered his band together for 45 minutes and, without saying a word, sang the refrain from a very old Wailers song, *Keep on Moving*.

130-131 Bob Marley in London in 1978 during an interview with the *Daily Mirror*. Marley released 12 albums. The compilation *Legend*, which came out three years after his death, is the one that has sold the most copies in the history of reggae: 25 million.

132 and 132-133 1 July 1980: Bob Marley performing at the Brighton Leisure Centre during his Uprising Tour. His last concert was on 23 September 1980 at the Stanley Theater in Pittsburgh, Pennsylvania. An article on state funerals in Jamaica appeared in the 22 May 1981 issue of the *New York Times* titled: "With Pride and Music, Jamaicans Bury Bob Marley."

134-135 1978: Bob Marley performs at the Santa Monica Civic Auditorium in California.

"WITH PRIDE AND MUSIC, JAMAICANS BURY BOB MARLEY"

[The New York Times]

JOHN
BELUSHI

[24 January 1949 > 5 March 1982]

At a very early age John Adam Belushi had three passions: baseball, theatre and rock 'n' roll. The son of an Albanian immigrant restaurateur, John had been born in Chicago, his family later relocating to Wheaton, about 25 miles from Chicago. His career began at the age of 22, when he joined the Second City Comedy, a Chicago theatre company specialising in improvised comedy sketches. There Belushi would take over and exaggerate the eccentricities of famous people and characters, such as Hamlet, the mayor of Chicago or Joe Cocker, and he always stole the show. His comic talent was immense, as was his uninhibited lifestyle. John Belushi was a unique cross between the transgressive rock 'n' roll myth and Hollywood decadence. He himself unwittingly predicted his own fate during a TV show on 17 December 1977 by wisecracking: "I plan to be dead by the time I'm 30." Before appearing on TV, John Belushi had demonstrated his prodigious talent, in 1971, by participating in the *National Lampoon Lemming*, an offshoot of the comic magazine "National Lampoon," with a takeoff of the Woodstock festival. The show launched Chevy Chase's career, but the audience went wild over Belushi's impersonation of Joe Cocker. When someone once asked him how he managed to be so relaxed on stage, he replied: "The stage is the only place where I really know what I'm doing." During that period he met another comic actor who would become his perfect foil, Dan Aykroyd. In 1973 Belushi moved to New York, with his future wife Judy Jacklin, and became part of the cast of the radio program *The National Lampoon Radio Hour*. Two years later he appeared on *Saturday Night Live* – the cult TV program created by Lorne Michaels – in an irresistible parody of American culture and politics. Belushi was quite sceptical about TV and hadn't wanted to take part but had been finally persuaded by his friend Gilda Radner. Similarly, the show's producers had nurtured some doubts about Belushi, as they were convinced he would only end up creating problems for them. But his participation proved to be a huge success. Later, Belushi's manic behaviour became a problem as he began to consume drugs and become uncontrollable. In fact, as Dan Aykroyd later related, when the *Saturday Night Live* rehearsals, shows or film shoots were finished John would often be in a state of utter exhaustion and would go friends' homes, or even strangers' homes, searching for food and sometimes even falling asleep on the spot. When that happened it became quite a job to find him and take him to work the next day.

His lifestyle corresponded with that of his first important cinema role: John Blutarsky, a symbol of demented rebellious youth in John Landis' film *Animal House*. But it was to be a sketch on *Saturday Night Live* that would establish him as a contemporary legend: on 22 April 1978 John

136-137 John Belushi in the role of Jake Blues at the Winterland Ballroom in San Francisco in 1978. One of his most famous quips was "If you think no one cares if you're alive, try not paying the installments on your car for two months."

Belushi and Dan Aykroyd went on the air, for the first time on NBC, as Joliet and Elwood Blues, the Blues Brothers. The inspiration for those characters had come to Aykroyd from a band in his hometown of Ottawa, Canada, the Downchild Blues Band, consisting of the brothers Donnie and Richard Walsh. Belushi, on the other hand, was overwhelmed by the blues during the filming of *Animal House* at Eugene, Oregon: one evening, in a night club, he met the 25 year-old singer and harmonist Curtis Salgado, and after talking about music with him for hours he had gone on stage with him to sing Floyd Dixon's *Hey Bartender*. That marked the beginning of a truly epic-making phenomenon. The Blues Brothers revived Chicago's electric blues and Memphis soul music with the album *Briefcase of Blues* (with the participation of Steve Cropper and Donald Duck Dunn of Booker T. & the M.G.'s) and in 1980 *The Blues Brothers*, directed by John Landis became one of the most successful movies in the history of cinema.

The story of the two blood brothers (who, according to the back cover of *Briefcase of Blues*, make their pact by cutting their middle finger with the string of a guitar that had once belonged to Elmore James) on a mission from God to save the orphanage where they had grown up and learned to play the blues, became a worldwide sensation. The cast included such legendary musicians as Cab Calloway, Aretha Franklin, James Brown, John Lee Hooker and Ray Charles, as well as many stars in cameo roles: Chaka Khan, Twiggy, Frank Oz, Joe Walsh (the Eagles guitarist) and Steven Spielberg. The movie has gone down in history partly because it holds the record for most cars destroyed during shooting and it even earned praise from the official Vatican newspaper "L'Osservatore Romano." That was the high point of John Belushi's career. Between 1979 and 1981 he acted in three other highly successful comic movies, *1941, Neighbors* and *Continental Divide*. But his unbridled, self-destructive nature finally drew him to an inevitable end. He had quipped that he would be dead by the age of 30. He was a hardened smoker and drinker, and also used amphetamines, cocaine and heroin. In the latter part of his life Belushi had become very overweight. He once said that the message his characters conveyed was that it was all right to screw up. In his opinion people didn't necessarily have to be perfect, nor did they have to follow rules; the important thing was to enjoy oneself. He had added that most present-day movies make people feel inadequate, but his did not do so.

His demise was spectacular and dramatic. It took place in the most uninhibited and decadent place in the world, Hollywood. On 5 March 1982 his personal trainer, karate champion Bill Wallace, went to pick him up in what had been his house for the past few days, bungalow number three in the Chateau Marmont Hotel on Sunset Boulevard. He found him dead.

Belushi's last night was a mystery of an uncontrolled spiral of self-indulgence that made him a legendary figure. Indeed, the saga of his rise and fall tended to obscure his extraordinary comic talent and the fact that he was an excellent singer. He had been in his bungalow, furiously drinking and taking drugs while

138-139 The Blues Brothers recording their debut album, *Briefcase Full of Blues* (1978) during a show when they were back-up to comedian Steve Martin, in Los Angeles. The album topped the American Billboard charts, sold 2 million copies and led to the success of the cover of a song by Sam & Dave, *Soul Man*.

receiving many of his friends, including author Nelson Ryan and actors Robin Williams and Robert De Niro. And there had also been Cathy Smith, a groupie, vocalist and the stars' favourite pusher. Her career in the dark side of rock music had begun in the 1960s with a relationship with Levon Helm of The Band, continued with Canadian vocalist Gordon Lightfoot and had ended in the late 1970s, when she had provided Ron Wood and Keith Richards with their stash of heroin. Belushi had met Cathy Smith on the set of *Saturday Night Live*, in 1976. The night of 5 March 1982 he called her and invited her to his place in the Chateau Marmont. A few hours later he had died from an injection of speedball, a mixture of cocaine and heroin. On 29 June 1982 Cathy Smith gave an interview to the *National Enquirer* with the title "I Killed John Belushi." She confessed that she had been the one to inject the fatal dose of speedball. She escaped to Canada, where she remained until she was extradited to the United States in 1986, where she pleaded guilty to a charge of involuntary manslaughter and was sentenced to 15 months in prison. John Belushi lies at rest in the Abel's Hill Cemetery in Martha's Vineyard, Massachusetts. His funeral was opened by Dan Aykroyd seated on his motorcycle and dressed in black. His friend James Taylor sang *That Lonesome Road*. Carved on his tombstone is the following: "I may be gone but rock 'n' roll lives on."

140-141 10 March 1982: Dan Aykroyd at John Belushi's funeral at the West Tisbury Congregational Church in Martha's Vineyard, Massachusetts. Belushi had died three days before in bungalow number three of the Chateau Marmont hotel in Hollywood.

141 6 March 1982: the front page of the *Chicago Tribune* announces the death of John Belushi.

JAMES HONEYMAN-SCOTT

[4 November 1956 > 16 June 1982]

PETE FARNDON

[12 June 1952 > 14 April 1983]

Success is quickly consumed. The rock 'n' roll fable of Chrissie Hynde, the singer and leader of the Pretenders, is closely connected with the tragic story of two members of her band, guitarist James Honeyman-Scott and bass guitarist Pete Farndon. Everything had happened so rapidly. Chrissie Hynde had come from Ohio and had arrived in London in 1973, where she first worked as a waitress, then as a journalist for the UK music magazine NME (the New Musical Express) and finally as a shop assistant in Malcolm McLaren's and Vivienne Westwood's clothing store SEX. In 1978 she formed The Pretenders with Martin Chambers, James Honeyman-Scott and Pete Farndon. They recorded a demo with five songs, including the cover of a Kinks song, *Stop Your Sobbing*. The band had no name at that time, so Chrissie Hynde chose The Pretenders, inspired by , *The Great Pretender*, by The Platters. *Stop Your Sobbing* was released in 1979 and was an immediate success.

It was followed by their debut album, *Pretenders*, promoted by the single *Brass in Pocket*, and the band became number one in the UK charts.

In 1981, during the band's first tour of America, Chrissie met, of all people, Ray Davies of the Kinks and married him, and in the meantime the band's second album, *Pretenders II*, was being released. While her life was becoming a rock fable, Pete Farndon's health had been deteriorating. Pete Farndon was addicted to heroin and it had become impossible to continue to play with him. After the final date of their world tour, in Bangkok, The Pretenders came to a decision: Pete Farndon had to leave the band. His friend James Honeyman-Scott had been given the task of telling him the bad news. James flew from Austin, Texas (where he had a home with his wife) to London, and on 14 June 1982 had told Farndon that he had been dismissed – Farndon disappeared without trace for two days. Then Chrissie Hynde received a phone call telling her that the corpse

of a member of her band was in a friend's house. "Is it Pete?" she had asked. "No, it's James," came the reply. James Honeyman-Scott had died of heart failure due to cocaine intolerance. He had been 25 and his unique sound had already influenced a host of guitarists, including Johnny Marr of The Smiths. Less than a year later, on 14 April 1983, Pete Farndon's wife found him drowned in their bathtub. It had been a final dose of heroin.

The fairy tale of The Pretenders had become a tragedy in only three years. Chrissie Hynde disappeared from the scene for a year and then re-formed the band, which returned to the charts with the single *Back on the Chain Gang*, and then released the album *Learning To Crawl*. In the lyrics Chrissie related her entire life, the pain of ending a love affair and the fear of becoming an adult. And, how difficult it had been to leave behind two friends and two talents like James Honeyman-Scott and Pete Farndon.

143 The Pretenders in London in 1979. From left to right, James Honeyman-Scott, Chrissie Hynde, Pete Farndon and Martin Chambers. The band was formed in Hereford, England, in March 1978.

DENNIS WILSON

"Brian Wilson is the Beach Boys. We're just his messengers. He's everything, we're nothing," Dennis Wilson had once said. Dennis had been the dark horse and black sheep of the band that sang about the California sun, the Beach Boys, the boy who gained wealth and fame in a band founded by his brothers Carl and Brian. The band had also been his passport to a frenetic life marked by drug and alcohol abuse, a considerable number of women (he married and divorced five times, twice to the same woman and his last wife was 19 year-old Shawn Marie Love, the "illegitimate" daughter of his cousin Mike Love), and dangerous friendships. A life seemingly destined for tragedy and that, in fact, ended at the age of 39 in Marina del Rey, California. That was the fate of the only true surfer in the Beach Boys, the one who had suggested exploiting the great popularity of surfing by making it the Beach Boys' theme.

In 1959, with the release of the film *Gidget* starring Sandra Dee, surfing had become an integral part of mass culture. Two years later, in a house in Hawthorne, the Beach Boys were formed by Brian and Carl Wilson, their cousin Mike Love and Al Jardine. At first Dennis had been excluded from the band, originally called The Pendletons, because his voice had not been as good as the others', but their mother Audree insisted. Their first recording was a cover of an old folk tune, *Sloop John B*, then Dennis suggested to Brian and Mike that they write a song about the new sport and lifestyle that were becoming so popular along the California ocean front, where he had been spending most of his time. The song was called *Surfin'*. The Beach Boys gave their first performance during a show featuring Ike and Tina Turner, at Long Beach on New Year's Eve in 1961. The following year they signed a contract with Capitol Records and released their first album, *Surfin' Safari*. Three more albums came out in 1963: *Surfin' USA*, *Surfer Girl* and *Little Deuce Coupe*, and they set

a record of sixteen hit singles in the following two years, which made them the most important band in the United States. Dennis Wilson played drums for the band until 1972, when a hand injury forced him to stop (he was replaced by Ricky Fataar), after which he played the piano and wrote some of the songs on the new Beach Boys album, *Sunflower*, which included his most famous song, *Forever*. Dennis also became the first band member to create a solo album, *Pacific Ocean Blue* (1977). But, after that his voice rapidly deteriorated due to alcohol and fast living as well as too many women: besides being the only surfer in the band, Dennis was also the most handsome. A series of questionable love affairs had led to his coming into contact with, and even befriending, sinister figures such as Charles Manson. One spring day in 1968, Dennis had picked up two hitchhikers, Ella Jo Bailey and Patricia Krenwinkel. He had taken them to his house on Sunset Boulevard, slept with both of them, and had then gone on to a recording session. When he returned, he found the house occupied by Charles Manson and his so-called Family, who all stayed with him for months, a period marked by orgies and experiments with psychedelic drugs. Dennis spent a fortune keeping this wild partying going and didn't seem to have been too worried about what was happening. He was a huge spendthrift, so much so that near the end of his career he was excluded from the groupband's earnings. He also helped Charles Manson to realise his dream of becoming a rock star. He took him to the recording studio with the Beach Boys, got him an audition with producer Terry Melcher (which was a flop) and persuaded Brian Wilson to record one of Manson's songs, originally *Cease to Exist* but released as *Never Learn Not to Love*. Then the relationship between the two friends of that summer on Sunset Boulevard suddenly worsened. The presence of the "Family" in Dennis Wilson's house became more and more awkward and even

145 Dennis Wilson was the rock 'n' roll element of the Beach Boys as well as the only true surfer in the group: "I don't know why everybody doesn't live at the beach, on the ocean. It makes no sense to me, hanging around the dirty, ugly-as-shit city. That's why I always loved and was proud to be a Beach Boy; I always loved the image. On the beach, you can live in bliss."

dangerous. Manson went so far as to threaten to rape Wilson's girlfriend Croxey Adams. The Beach Boys included *Never Learn Not to Love* on their album *20/20* (1969) which they also released as a single (with the single *Bluebirds Over the Mountain* on the B-side) which went to 61st place in the American charts). Manson had been furious at the change of song title. Dennis Wilson was afraid of him and solved the problem, simply, by annulling the rental contract and leaving the owners with the unpleasant task of evicting the "Family." Manson sent him an envelope containing a hysterical message and a bullet!

9 August 1969 was the date of the massacre at Cielo Drive (the villa rented by Roman Polanski and Sharon Tate and owned by Terry Melcher, who Manson blamed for cutting short his career), after which Dennis Wilson refused to talk about his strange relationship with Manson and his "Family." In the 1970s he had continued to be the black sheep of the Beach Boys, enjoying a huge success with his debut solo album *Pacific Ocean Blue* (1977). But he continued to drink and to squander his

money, ending up bankrupt. He was also reluctant to seriously try to break free of his alcohol dependence. On 28 December 1983 he was invited to a friend's boat moored in Marina del Rey. He had also once owned a boat, a 62 foot yacht called *Harmony*, which he had had to sell. He had just ended one of his many attempts to break free from his alcohol dependence, but had begun drinking early that morning. It was a typical party with his friends. At 3.00 pm he decided to have a swim and dived into the cold water. He resurfaced with a framed photograph of his former wife, Karen Lamm, that he had thrown into the water, from *Harmony*, years earlier during an argument. Despite his friends' objections he dived in several more times, stating that he wanted to recover other objects from the seabed. The final time he never resurfaced. His body was recovered at 5.30 am. A combination of prescribed medication, alcohol and cocaine had led to his premature death at the age of 39. The Beach Boy who loved the sea and surfing had ended his life in water and his death marked the end of the band.

146 Dennis Wilson performing live with the Beach Boys in 1976. From 1972 to 1974, due to an injury to one of his hands, he was temporarily replaced by Ricky Fataar. Wilson returned to the drum set after the release of the Beach Boys compilation *Endless Summer*.

147 top The Beach Boys during a concert in California in 1964. From left to right, Dennis Wilson, Al Jardine, Carl Wilson, Brian Wilson and Mike Love.

147 bottom *The Standard* reports the news of Dennis Wilson's death: "Beach Boys Star Drowns in Freezing Ocean after Drinking All Day."

MARVIN
GAYE

A sudden shot shattered the silence at Gramercy Place, Los Angeles. It was 1 April 1984, when an absurd outbreak of violence ended the life of the greatest soul singer in the world, a man with the voice of an angel and as handsome as a god: Marvin Gaye. He was killed a day before his 45th birthday. He had been shot and killed by his father, Reverend Marvin Pentz Gay Sr.

This was the epilogue to a family tragedy that never seemed to end. Marvin Gaye was one of the most talented and visionary musicians in the history of music, a sublime and doomed figure. He was an artist who not only redefined soul music with his songs, but also interpreted it as a powerful catalyst for change in society. Yet all his artistic tension derived from continuous inner torment that triggered a conflicting relationship between him and his father. His biographer, Steve Turner, wrote that Gaye wanted to die but couldn't manage to do it himself. That was why he virtually drove his father to kill him. What were the roots of that story, that reads like a Greek tragedy?

Marvin was the second of three children of Alberta and Reverend Gay Sr. He was born in Washington D.C. on 2 April 1939. His father was as a strict minister of the House of God, a religious sect that merged elements of orthodox Judaism and the Pentecostal Movement, and he was convinced that part of his mission was to impose Old Testament teachings on his family, by force if necessary. He was also an alcoholic and often punished other family members while wearing

women's clothing. Marvin was the rebellious son who would not accept such absolute control and grew up amidst violence and beatings. But he was also extremely gifted musically and his talent was revealed when he sang in the church choir at the age of three.

His career began in the doo-wop group The Rainbows, with whom he released the single *Wyatt Earp* and in 1958 joined the Harvey Fuqua's band, The Moonglows. Marvin moved to Chicago, recorded some singles for Chess Records and then toured the Midwest. During a concert in Detroit he was noticed by the founder of Motown Records, Berry Gordy, who put him under contract in 1961. Marvin began as a session drummer for Smokey Robinson but very soon his voice convinced Gordy to launch him as a soloist. His first single success was *Stubborn Kind of Fellow* (1962) and from that time Marvin recorded 39 hits, either by himself or singing with Mary Wells or Kim Weston, becoming the Motown star. His relationship with the label became even stronger when Marvin married Anna Gordy, Berry Gordy's sister, in 1961.

His brilliant career continued with his duets with Tammi Terrell and the great success of *I Heard It through the Grapevine* (1968) which marked the high point of the splendid Motown sound. Yet from the outset, shadows were lurking behind his success. Marvin was not pleased with his role as a pop singer; he wanted to employ soul language and style to address and describe the social changes and reality of his time. Furthermore,

he was shattered by an incident that occurred in 1967 during a concert in Virginia: Tammi Terrell had collapsed in his arms on stage. It had been the first sign a brain tumour that ultimately killed her on 16 March 1970. Marvin Gaye was overwhelmed with grief over the death of his partner. He said he no longer wanted to sing duos and withdrew from live performances, working alone on an album that became one of the great masterpieces of contemporary popular music, *What's Going On* (1971). It was an inspired and conceptual album that definitively broke down the divisions between black and white music by combining jazz, funk and Latin soul and became a model thanks to its themes: the controversial social issues and demands of the time. Marvin formulated the songs in keeping with the perspective of his brother Frankie, who had just returned from Vietnam, and it dealt with such subjects as poverty, war and political corruption.

That was the moment when he was recognised as one of the music greats. Yet his private life was falling apart. His marriage was in trouble and Marvin was having an affair with 17 year-old Janice Hunter, to whom he dedicated *Let's Get It On* (1973). The divorce marked the beginning of a downward spiral in his life. Marvin Gaye continued to enjoy success with an album of duets with Diana Ross and the album *I Want You* (1976) but he was in financial difficulty and could not pay his former wife's alimony. So he was forced to cut another album to pay his debts. The album, *Here My Dear*

149 Marvin Gaye's debut single, *Let Your Conscience Be Your Guide*, was released in May 1961. The last one, *Joy*, taken from the album *Midnight Love*, was released in 1983. In 2008 *Rolling Stone* ranked him number six on its Greatest Singers of All Time list.

(1978), was a depiction of his bitter relationship with Anna. And then there was his addiction to drugs, especially cocaine, which the singer consumed irrepressibly. Unpaid taxes, alimony, contract obligations, disputes with Motown and cocaine. And above it all, the shadow of his father, who had never loved him and considered his success to be offensive. And it was precisely his career that had allowed Marvin to support the entire family, thus depriving his father of his role as absolute head of the household. And that career continued in an increasingly desperate spiral of dependence. Marvin fell victim to paranoia and sexual obsessions. In 1979, after a concert in Hawaii, he had remained there as he was afraid he would be imprisoned for tax evasion if he returned to the continental United States. In 1981 he went to Europe for a series of concerts, in order to pay his debts and the following year he left Motown and signed a contract with Columbia Records. By 1982 matters seemed to be improving thanks to the success of the single *Sexual Healing* taken from the album *Midnight Love*. Thanks to that song he became a star once again. The following year he was reconciled with Berry Gordy, during the celebration of Motown's anniversary, and he captivated the American public with a deeply moving interpretation of the national anthem at the NBA All Star Game. But those were his final public appearances. Hounded by his demons and more and more dependent upon cocaine, Marvin returned to the United States and took refuge at his parent's home in Los Angeles.

Father and son lived together but hated each other. Reverend Gay told his son that he was the Devil Incarnate and Marvin, in turn, constantly provoked him, even going so far as to give him a pistol. He would stay for days on end in his room, watching pornographic films and sniffing cocaine, while his many fans remained outside the house and shouted his name. Marvin Gaye was dragged down by a mysterious power and he seemed to have decided to die by exorcizing his relationship with his father. His mother Alberta stated: "His father didn't kill him, Marvin committed suicide."

The tragic event took place on the morning of 1 April 1984. There had been another of the usual fights, Marvin attacked his father and hit him, his mother managed to separate them and took her son back to his room. A short while later, Reverend Gay entered the room, holding the pistol his

son had given him. He shot him twice and Marvin fell to the floor. His father was sentenced to five years probation and had to live in a rest home in Inglewood. The judge decided that the victim had provoked his own death with his aggressive behaviour. "I don't make records for pleasure," Gaye had said in a 1982 interview. "I did when I was a younger artist, but I don't today. I record so that I can feed people what they need, what they feel. Hopefully, I record so that I can help someone overcome a bad time."

150 top April 1984: a handcuffed Reverend Marvin Gay Sr. is taken away by the Los Angeles police after killing his son.

150 bottom The front page of the 2 April 1984 issue of *The Standard* announces Gaye's death. The newspaper also published a declaration by his father about why he shot his son.

150-151 Marvin Gaye in his Los Angeles home in 1982.

CLIFF
BURTON

[10 February 1962 > 27 September 1986]

Dörarp is a rural town in the district of Ljungby in southern Sweden. It is traversed by the European Route 4 highway, which runs almost the entire length of the east coast of Sweden, from Finland. On 27 September 1986 it became the site of a tragedy that struck the most important thrash metal band in the world, Metallica. At 7.00 am the band's tour bus skidded off the road and turned over in a ditch. The band members and the crew were all asleep after a late concert at Stockholm's Solnahallen Arena. Metallica were promoting their third album, the one that marked a turning point in their creative approach, *Master of Puppets*. A cascade of powerful thrash metal that earned them 29th place in the US charts and led to their first gold certification. Metallica were ready to conquer the world of heavy metal. But that morning, on a country road in Sweden, an absurd accident ended the life of their bass guitarist, Clifford Lee "Cliff" Burton. When the bus overturned Cliff was thrown out of a window and was crushed by the vehicle. He and guitarist Kirk Hammett had drawn cards to see who would get the most comfortable bunk bed. A cursed card, the ace of spades, marked his fate.

Cliff Burton was born in Castro Valley, California, on 10 February 1962. He began to play the bass guitar when he was 13, after his brother's death: "I want to become the best bass guitarist in the world for him," he told his parents. By practising up to six hours a day he developed a remarkable technique and, in 1982, became a member of his first major band, Trauma. James

Hetfield and Lars Ulrich, who had formed Metallica a year earlier, discovered Cliff during a concert at the Whisky a Go Go club in Los Angeles. He was so talented that not only did the band members ask him to take Ron McGovern's place but also decided to relocate to the town of El Cerrito because Cliff didn't want to leave the San Francisco Bay Area. Burton demonstrated his great technical skill on *(Anesthesia) Pulling Teeth*, which was on Metallica's first album, *Kill 'Em All*. He also wrote six of the eight songs on their next album, *Ride the Lightning*, thanks to which the band was offered a contract with Elektra Records, where they recorded, arguably, their best album, *Master of Puppets*. They then went on a long US tour with rocker Ozzy Osbourne and, on 17 March 1986, arrived in Europe for their Damage Inc. Tour, which continued until the accident at Dörarp. Seven ambulances took the injured to Ljungby hospital, but nothing could be done for Cliff Burton.

Was this an accident or a case of distraction? Kirk Hammett, who was tormented by the fateful card draw he and Cliff had played to win the best bed on the bus, has always stated that the driver smelled of alcohol and no evidence of ice was found on the road. The Swedish police arrested the driver and charged him with manslaughter but released him a few days later. Metallica continued their rise to fame in the heavy metal sphere with a new bass guitarist, Jason Newsted and Cliff Burton, who wanted to be the best bass guitarist in the world, became a legend.

153 Clifton Lee Burton on stage during his 1986 promotional tour of Metallica's third album, *Master of Puppets*. Lars Ulrich had the following to say about him: "Cliff Burton was the man who had that wild spirit that makes a band like Metallica a quality band."

154-155 Metallica in 1985: Kirk Hammett, James Hetfield, Lars Ulrich and Cliff Burton. In 1988 the band paid a tribute to Cliff with the instrumental piece *To Live Is To Die* released on the album *...And Justice For All*.

PETER TOSH

[19 October 1944
> 11 September 1987]

"Don't care where you come from. As long as you're a black man you're an African." Peter Tosh was a warrior of music. His nom de guerre was Steppin' Razor, a reggae soldier who sang against injustice in Jamaica and throughout the world. Peter was the one who taught his friend Bob Marley to play the guitar down at Trenchtown, the Kingston ghetto. Winston Hubert McIntosh (his real name) arrived in Kingston from the Grange Hill countryside when he was 15 years old. He was the illegitimate son of a woman who was too young to take care of him and he was raised by his aunt. Tosh taught himself to play the guitar and attended free lessons from singing teacher Joe Higgs.

This is the beginning of the story of the most powerful Jamaican band, The Wailers. In 1962 Peter Tosh, Bob Marley and Bunny Wailer sang at street corners in Trenchtown, drawing inspiration from Curtis Mayfield's band The Impressions, then they met Junior Braithwaite, Beverley Kelso and Cherry Smith and, in 1964, formed The Wailing Wailers, which debuted with the ska single *Simmer Down*. In 1966 Marley spent a year in the United States, where he worked in a Chrysler automobile factory in Delaware, and when he returned to Jamaica he found that Tosh and Wailer had embraced the Rastafari religion and were involved in supporting the cause of the poor in their country. Peter Tosh had already recorded two songs, *I'm the Toughest* and *Rasta Shook Them Up*. However, ska rhythm was no longer suitable for expressing the band's political message, so Tosh, Wailer and Marley formed a new band with brothers Aston "Family Man" Barrett and Carlton Barrett, changing the name to The Wailers. In the meantime, their meeting with the legendary producer Lee "Scratch" Perry gave rise to a new sound, reggae, which brought Jamaican music to the attention of the whole world. In 1973 The Wailers signed a contract with Chris

Blackwell's Island Records and released *Catch a Fire* and *Burnin'*. Reggae became the voice of people fighting for their rights and Marley became a major figure in the history of music, the first Third World super star. Tosh remained a militant at his side, a warrior struggling against the so-called Babylonian system, which he called the "shit-stem." His inner torment was analogous to Marley's. Their common denominators were talent and an irrepressible rebellious instinct. But, whereas Marley was inspired and spiritual, Tosh was violent and unpredictable. His interpretation of reggae was radical, armed to the teeth, so to speak, and left no margin whatsoever for dialogue with the Babylonian system, in true Jamaican style. The heart of his music was not the universal message that Marley expressed in *One Love* but the cry of rebellion in *Get Up, Stand Up*. And his violent life became a symbol of the struggle of a people that had never tolerated bowing before the powers that be.

Tosh made his debut as a solo artist in 1976 with *Legalize It*, an album that was so explicit that it was even censored in Jamaica because of its anti-drug prohibition message, which made him a kind of public enemy. The most spectacular example of his militant behaviour was the One Love Peace Concert of 26 February 1978, organised by Bob Marley to bring about reconciliation in Jamaica, which, at the time, was ravaged by a civil war between supporters of the prime minister, Michael Manley, and the opposition Jamaican Labour Party of Edward Saga. On stage that night were the most important Jamaican reggae artists, from the Inner Circle to Dennis Brown. Bob Marley was in a state of trance and he got the two rivals to shake hands to the notes of *Jamming* stating: "If we want our dreams to come true we must stay united." Peter Tosh, on the other hand, smoked a joint on stage and violently attacked the two leaders for their

157 Winston Hubert McIntosh, better known as Peter Tosh, in 1970. After leaving the Wailers in 1976, Tosh released *Legalize It*, which was followed by *Equal Rights*, *Bush Doctor*, *Mystic Man*, *Wanted Dread and Alive*, *Mama Africa* and *No Nuclear War*.

repressive policy toward the *sufferah* of the ghetto and toward marijuana consumption.

The battle had just begun. Four months later, on his way back home after an evening at the Skateland Dance Hall in Kingston, he was seized by the police, who beat him savagely and left him at death's door. This was the revenge of Babylon, with which Tosh was only too familiar: earlier, in 1972, following a police raid on his home, he woke up on the floor of the Kingston Public Hospital surrounded by policemen who prevented the physicians from taking care of him. His second album, *Equal Rights* (1977), was a manual of militant music, and apart from a new version of *Get Up, Stand Up* and his anthem *Steppin' Razor* (a song by Joe Higgs that he had previously recorded in 1967), it contained *African, Equal Rights* and *Apartheid,* three of the most powerful songs, exhorting social justice, in the history of reggae.

One of the first persons to be fascinated by Tosh's spirit was Mick Jagger, who put him under contract to Rolling Stones Records. From 1978 to 1981 Tosh released *Bush Doctor, Mystic Man* and *Wanted Dread And Alive.*

Despite this help from the Rolling Stones, the attempt to reach a larger audience while remaining true to his ideas succeeded only partially. Yet he did not stop conveying his message: in 1983 he signed a contract with EMI, released the album *Mama Africa* and departed on what would be his last tour, which ended in Kingston on 30 December 1983. However, every step of his career was like a battle. Tosh opposed the distribution of his albums in South Africa, accused EMI of not promoting him enough, and left the music scene for a few years. In 1987 his career seemed to take off once again with *No Nuclear War,* which earned him a Grammy Award for the best reggae performance. But, at that stage, Tosh confessed he was bankrupt and was thinking of making a tour to solve his financial problems.

However, his plan was cut short by another night of violence in the life of a renegade. On 11 September 1987, Peter was celebrating his return to Jamaica, in his home in the St. Andrew district of Kingston, with his wife Marlene Brown and some friends, the musicians Carlton "Santa" Davis and Michael Robinson and one of his many healers, the herbalist Wilton Doc Brown. Tosh was waiting for another guest, the DJ Jeff Dixon and his wife Joy. The doorbell rang. Michael Robinson opened the door and found three armed men on the porch. One was Dennis "Leppo" Lobban, a Kingston gangster whom Tosh had helped on many occasions by offering him hospitality and money. He was a ghetto sufferah to whom the Rasta warrior had offered a chance to escape his condition as a slave of Babylon.

The circumstances of that cursed night are mysterious. Why did Lobban decide to attack his friend of all people? "Where's the money?" he asked him in fury. Tosh replied that there was no money in his house and tried to make Dennis listen to reason. At this stage Jeff and Joy Dixon rang the doorbell. The thugs let them in, pointing their pistols at them. The thieves continued to ask Tosh where his money was. Then violence suddenly exploded: shots were fired, one of which grazed Marlene Brown and hit Joy Dixon in the face. Lobban lost control, pointed his pistol at Tosh and killed him with two shots in the forehead. The other two thieves opened fire and killed Wilton Brown and Jeff Dixon. Marlene Brown managed to escape and give the alarm, but it was too late. Peter Tosh, the warrior Steppin' Razor, died at the age of 43.

The mystery of what seemed nothing more or less than an execution continued. Dennis Lobban was tried on 17 July 1988 and sentenced to death; yet he declared he was innocent. His two accomplices were never identified and it is said they were killed in a gang fight. On 21 July Lobban's death sentence was commuted to life imprisonment. He had always said he had been framed and that that night he was not in St. Andrews. Many questions remain unanswered. But one thing is certain: the death of public enemy Peter Tosh in Jamaica was in the "best interests" of many people.

159 Peter Tosh during a 1975 concert: "I travel the garden of music, thru inspiration. It's a large, very large garden."

160-161 29 June 1981: Peter Tosh during a concert at the Rainbow Theatre in London.

JACO

PASTORIUS

Talent and torment. Jaco Pastorius is the symbol of how mental disorder might increase a musician's creativity yet also destroy his life. At 13 Jaco had begun to play the drums, like his father Jack who had been a 'big band' drummer, but he had had to quit soon after because he had injured his wrist during a football game. He then bought his first electric bass guitar, for 15 dollars, and began to learn to play. At that time he had already been playing as the drummer with a local band, Las Olas Brass, at Oakland Park, Fort Lauderdale, Florida. In 1969 he purchased a Fender Jazz bass, an instrument that would make him a legendary figure. Jaco Pastorius became a session musician for various rhythm & blues and jazz bands and, in 1974, collaborated with Pat Metheny on his album *Bright Size Life*. But it was to be his solo debut that would make history: in 1976 the album *Jaco Pastorius* was released and established him as the best bass player in the world. Such prestigious musicians as Herbie Hancock, Michael Brecker, Sam & Dave, and Wayne Shorter played along with him. When he met Weather Report's Josef Zawinul he introduced himself as follows: "I'm the greatest bass player in the world." Zawinul's first reaction had been to tell Jaco to close the door on his way out, but when he had listened to his work he asked him to take part in the recording of *Black Market*. Thanks to Pastorius, Weather Report became a jazz institution.

Pastorius left the band in 1981 to resume his solo career, but he began to show signs of mental illness: in 1982, in Japan, during the tour promoting his *Word of Mouth* album, he shaved his head, painted his face black and threw his bass guitar into Hiroshima Bay. Following the tour he was diagnosed with bipolar disorder (formerly known as manic depression), which was aggravated by alcohol abuse. Jaco was evicted from his New York apartment and began living on the streets before finally being placed in Bellevue Hospital for a time. He then returned to Florida, continuing to live on the streets of Fort Lauderdale for weeks at a time. Music had been his only salvation until 21 September 1987, the day that proved to be the last day of his life. Jaco had wanted to stop drinking, go back to performing and be reconciled with his girlfriend Teresa. He had borrowed some money from his brother Gregory and had invited Teresa out to a Thai restaurant for dinner: "If he hadn't died," Teresa said later, "I would have gone back to him." Jaco telephoned his friend Carlos Santana and asked him for free tickets to his concert at the Sunrise Music Theater. Everything had seemed to be going well, but once again his demons got the best of him. Jaco had begun drinking, then he had jumped onto the stage and was thrown out of the hall. By now totally drunk, he insulted Teresa and went to another club where he jammed with some friends and was, again, thrown off the premises. He persuaded another friend, Ricky Hurt, to take him to the Midnight Bottle Club at Wilton Manors to see Gary Carter's band, where, on being refused entry, he reportedly kicked in a glass door and had a fight with one of the club's security men, Luc Havan, suffering facial fractures and other injuries which caused him to be hospitalised. At 4.43 am an ambulance took Pastorius to the Broward General Medical Center. The doctors told Jaco's father Jack that he might pull through but that he would lose his right eye and the use of his left arm. Jaco Pastorius was in a coma for ten days and never regained consciousness. Luc Havan pleaded guilty to manslaughter and was sentenced to 22 months in prison with five years probation. He was released from prison four months later. The day Jaco Pastorius died the music world lost one of the best musicians of all time.

163 John Francis Pastorius III was born in Norristown, Pennsylvania, on 1 December 1951 and grew up in Fort Lauderdale, Florida. He bought his first bass guitar for 15 dollars: "I use my instrument as if I were playing with a human voice. I play as if I were speaking, I like singers."

CHET
BAKER

[23 December 1929 > 13 May 1988]

   Chesney Henry Baker Jr., better known as Chet Baker, was 59 but seemed much older. His face
bore all the signs of a dissolute life, and years of heroin addiction, which had begun long before, in the
1950s. In 1978 he took refuge in Europe because so many people in the United States had forgotten the
trumpet playing that had represented great moments in the history of jazz. Chet Baker had played with
Stan Getz, Charlie Parker and Gerry Mulligan, he had released such a fundamental album as *Chet
Baker Sings* and had spent most of his musical life on tour. But heroin had brought him a lot of trouble.
He had spent a year in prison, in Italy, and had been expelled from Germany and the United Kingdom.
In 1966, after a concert held in San Francisco, he had been attacked by a gang of thieves who had
knocked out his front teeth so that for some time he had been unable to play the trumpet and had
ended up working in a service station. His physical and personal decline was described by Bruce Weber
in the documentary *Let's Get Lost*. Baker made several comebacks thanks to his prodigious talent.
In the ten years 1978 to 1988 he made 40 albums, the last one, *My Favorite Songs Vol. 1-2: The Last
Great Concert*, was released on 28 April 1988, only two weeks before his death. Elvis Costello re-
launched his career in 1983 by inviting him to play on the single *Shipbuilding*, which made the Top 40
in the British charts, while his 1987 tour of Japan is generally considered the apex of his career.
But drugs condemned him to constant physical and mental torment and led him to a mysterious end.
   On 13 May 1988, Chet Baker was in room 210 of the Hotel Prins Hendrik in Amsterdam, all alone.
A final leap from the window and his life ended in the street, where he had always lived. The Dutch
police found heroin and cocaine in his room and closed the case by reporting it as an accident. There
were no witnesses so no one really knows whether or not he committed suicide. Chet Baker is buried
in the Inglewood Park Cemetery in California. His music and his image as a doomed jazz artist remain
in the annals of music history.

166-167 Chet Baker performing at the Blue Note club in New York in 1974. This period was one of the many comebacks of a
tormented artist who gave jazz a huge body of recorded work and many profound emotions, beginning with his first great success,
My Funny Valentine, recorded in 1952 with the Gerry Mulligan Quartet.

168 and 169 Chet Baker's life was narrated by photographer Bruce Weber in the documentary *Let's Get Lost* (1988). Weber began to become interested in Chet Baker after seeing, in a Pittsburgh record shop, the cover of the album *Chet Baker Sings and Plays with Bud Shank, Russ Freeman and Strings* released in 1955.

HILLEL SLOVAK

[13 April 1962
> 25 June 1988]

"Hillel died too young. It could have happened to anyone in our scene. We made huge mistakes, but they grew out of love, and one mistake made us one less." Michael Balzary, better known as Flea, had been Hillel Slovak's buddy from the age of 12. They had met at Fairfax High School in Los Angeles. Hillel had taught Flea to play bass guitar, and when Flea became proficient Slovak had asked him to join his band, Anthym. Together they discovered music, drugs and the rock 'n' roll lifestyle, and in 1983, with Anthony Kiedis and Jack Irons they formed the band that created the sound that best represented the mad California spirit – the Red Hot Chili Peppers. Slovak later quit the Peppers to concentrate on his own band, What Is This? He rejoined the Peppers in 1985. Hillel Slovak had been the protagonist of, arguably, the Red Hot Chili Peppers' most famous song, *Under The Bridge,* in which Anthony Kiedis narrated the days he had spent with Hillel buying heroin from Mexican pushers under the freeway overpasses in the most notorious neighbourhoods of L.A. Heroin had deprived the music world of Hillel's talent and the guitar sound that had launched the Red Hot Chili Peppers with their albums *Freaky Styley* (1985) and *The Uplift Mofo Party Plan* (1987). "Hillel is the author of the sound we created," Anthony Kiedis once said. He had been the one who had defined that nervous and psychedelic funk sound that was to become the band's trademark and a point of reference for future bands. And he had also created the band's image. Until 1987 Hillel Slovak had been the Skinny Sweaty Man, from the title of one of the songs on the album *The Uplift Mofo Party Plan,* a brilliant guitarist who filled a stage with colourful clothes and maniacal dancing. A year later, however, he had become a mere shadow of his former self. Ironically, the band had been more worried about Anthony Kiedis's drug addiction, which was so noticeable and dangerous, to the extent that they didn't realise that Hillel had gone down the same one-way street. The first person to became concerned had been a roadie who, at the end of their European tour, had phoned Hillel's brother, James. Until that time no one in his family had had any inkling about Hillel's addiction. "It was a problem he knew he had to take care of, but he didn't do it," James Slovak had stated. "Heroin began as a creative and liberating experience and then turned into a four-year addiction totally out of control." James had promised not to say anything about it to their mother Esther, and Hillel had sworn that he wanted to become drug-free. He had been seeing a physician and had been taking medication. He and Anthony Kiedis had decided to try to stay clean together. On 21 January 1988 he had written in his diary that he had intended to start a new life. But during the ensuing months, when the band had taken a pause before beginning work on their fourth album, Hillel isolated himself more and more. On Saturday 25 June he bought some heroin and had shut himself up in his apartment in the Malaga Castle residential complex in Hollywood. He died of an overdose at some unspecified moment that same day. His body was found three days later by a friend, Keith Barry, who had been called by a neighbour, Bob Forrest. Hillel had been found lying on the last painting he had been working on. At 8.00 pm Barry and Forrest went to the home of James Slovak, who had spoken to Hillel only the day before. "Be careful, shooting heroin is like playing Russian roulette," James had told him. "I know, brother," Hillel had replied, "I love you." Hillel Slovak's funeral was held on 30 June at 1.00 pm at the Jewish cemetery, Mount Sinai Memorial Park. It was attended by his relatives, friends, colleagues and L.A. drug dealers. The only person missing was Anthony Kiedis, who could not cope with the idea that his friend had died and that he had not been there to help him. "It should have happened to me," he stated in a 1992 *Rolling Stone* interview. "I could tell that Hillel had no inner core of strength; his addiction had robbed him of the life force that allows you to at least defend yourself" he said.

171 The Red Hot Chili Peppers in 1985 during the recording sessions of their second album, *Freaky Styley:* from left to right, Anthony Kiedis, Cliff Martinez, Flea and Hillel Slovak. Slovak recorded a second album with the band, *The Uplift Mofo Party Plan* (1987). Flea said that Hillel was full of talent and opened freeways of creativity for Flea that he didn't think he even had.

PETE
DE FREITAS

[2 August 1961 > 14 June 1989]

The image that best described the life of Pete de Freitas was the video clip *China Doll* that Julian Cope realised in 1989: a mysterious motorcyclist arrives in town, conquers a girl then runs away with her. Pete de Freitas was the doomed hero of 1980s British rock music, an uninhibited drummer in love with motorcycles, who ended his trip through life on his Ducati in a terrible accident while racing to a recording studio in Liverpool. Before his tragic end, Pete was the soul of one of the bands that created a musical genre synonymous with a dark sentiment. The band was Echo & the Bunnymen, created in 1978, on stage at Eric's Club in Liverpool, by singer Ian McCulloch and guitarist Will Sergeant, who had chosen the name because, from the outset, they had played with a drum machine that they had called Echo. That same year bass guitarist Les Pattinson joined the band, which recorded its first single, *The Pictures on My Wall*, with Zoo, an independent label in Liverpool. In 1980 the band had decided to abandon the drum machine and had asked Pete de Freitas to become their drummer. Pete showed himself to be much more than a mere drummer. His tribal rhythms and heavy use of cymbals meshed perfectly with the reverb of Will Sergeant's guitar and soon became the backbone of the elegant and moody *Crocodiles*, released on 18 July 1980, and which put Echo & the

Bunnymen into the top 20 of the UK charts, followed by, *Heaven Up There* and *Porcupine*, which brought major success. The first great Echo & the Bunnymen hit was 1984's *The Killing Moon*, taken from *Ocean Rain*, recorded in Paris with the accompaniment of a 35-piece orchestra and universally considered the band's masterpiece.

But at the peak of his success Pete de Freitas left the band and went to New Orleans for two years, where he tried to launch a new band, The Sex Gods, only to end up overwhelmed by his excesses. After totalling two automobiles and two motorcycles and having set records in the unbridled rock 'n' roll lifestyle (it was rumoured that he had once stayed awake for 18 consecutive days and nights), Pete de Freitas had returned, penniless, to Liverpool in search of a second chance. Echo & The Bunnymen, which in the meantime had recorded an album by the same name, with former ABC drummer David Palmer, agreed to take him back but as a session drummer, on a salary. They then re-recorded the entire album. Released in 1987, it reached number four in the UK charts. However, the following year Ian McCulloch quit the band and de Freitas, Sergeant and Pattinson decided to continue as a trio, which they did – until that tragic accident which took the life of one of the best drummers of his generation.

173 Echo & The Bunnymen in 1985, after the release of their most famous album, *Ocean Rain*: Ian McCulloch, Pete De Freitas, Les Pattinson and Will Sergeant. De Freitas became a member of the 27 Club in 1989, when he lost his life in a motorcycle accident near Liverpool.

ANDREW
WOOD

[8 January 1966 > 19 March 1990]

Andrew Wood was the singer who put Seattle on the rock map, launching a scene that was destined to change the music of the 1990s forever. He was a flamboyant and fragile hero who idolised Freddie Mercury and, onstage, having chosen the stage name of Landrew the Love Child, wore makeup and costumes like those of Kiss. He would surely have become the first Seattle superstar had his life not been snuffed out at the age of 24.

Andrew Wood grew up in Bainbridge Island, Washington and when he was 14, with his brother Kevin, organised their first band, Malfunkshun. Attaining rock stardom was his purpose in life. He became Landrew the Love Child and followed the glam rock aesthetic, not only with his musical style but also by creating an indissoluble bond between life and art. Taking drugs was a way of drawing nearer to the gods of rock but a practice that, in 1985, led him to a rehab facility at the tender age of 19. Malfunkshun, which never released an album, became a point of reference for the Seattle music scene. Andrew's irresistible personality fascinated everyone and attracted musicians who then laid the groundwork for the so-called 'Seattle Sound', from Green River to Chris Cornell (who, at one time, shared an apartment with Andrew). In 1988, after Green River disbanded, he formed a new band, Mother Love Bone, with Jeff Ament and Stone Gossard of Green River. The following year the band released the EP *Shine* and began touring all year long, after which they returned to Seattle to record their first album, *Apple*.

This marked Andrew's step up to success. But, during his transformation into a superstar, he had to deal with a terrible enemy – heroin. He started serious rehab treatment in order to break free of heroin in time for the release of the album. Just a few days before the release date, 19 March 1990, he overdosed in his Seattle home and remained in a coma for three days, after which physicians called his relatives and friends and informed them that nothing more could be done for him. On 19 March 1990 life support was turned off. *Apple* was released on 19 July 1990 and was immediately acclaimed one of the most important rock albums of the 1990s. An offshoot of Mother Love Bone was a band of Seattle rock superstars – Pearl Jam.

174-175 Mother Love Bone in a 1990 photograph: far left is Andrew Wood. His death brought about the end of the band as well as the formation of two other historic grunge bands. His former roommate Chris Cornell formed a band in his honour, Temple of the Dog, while Stone Gossard and Jeff Ament (second and third from left) founded Pearl Jam.

174 Stevie Ray Vaughan recorded five albums that together sold 11.5 million copies and won six Grammy Awards. Eric Clapton said the following about Vaughan: "A lot of time will pass before we hear anything so extraordinary."

STEVIE RAY VAUGHAN

[3 October 1954 > 27 August 1990]

There was a guitarist who had been compared to Jimi Hendrix for his capacity to combine rock and blues – Jimmy Vaughan's younger brother, Stevie Ray Vaughan. For that matter, when he was very young Stevie spent hours playing his guitar, following note for note the records that Jimmy brought home, especially those featuring Hendrix, Buddy Guy, Muddy Waters and B.B. King, among others. And, when he was only ten years old, Stevie was already playing in his brother's band, Texas Storm, and then formed his own, Blackbird.

The Vaughans were greatly influenced by blues music. Jimmy left home when he was 15. Stevie worked as a dishwasher for less than a dollar an hour, then left school and moved to Austin, Texas with his Blackbird band. That marked the beginning of his career as a blues musician and he became one of the greatest interpreters of that genre during the 1980s. His new band, Double Trouble, was an institution on the Texas blues scene and in 1982 it was invited to the Montreux Jazz Festival, where Stevie's talent conquered two special guests, David Bowie and Jackson Browne. After hearing Stevie play, Bowie asked him to take part in the recordings of his album *Let's Dance*, and Browne offered him his Los Angeles studio, where Double Trouble cut their first album, *Texas Flood*, in less than a week. The almost simultaneous release of *Let's Dance* (number one on the American and British charts) and *Texas Flood*, in 1983, launched Stevie's career and he consolidated his reputation as a great bluesman with two more Double Trouble albums, *Couldn't Stand the Weather*, released in 1984, and *Soul to Soul*, released in 1985.

However, there was a problem. During the interminable tours with Double Trouble, Stevie entered a life-threatening spiral, becoming heavily addicted to alcohol and cocaine, so much so that it appeared that his life would become part of the legend of damned rock stars. He would consume as much as a quarter of an ounce of cocaine per day, as well as fifths of whisky and vodka. But fate had something else in store for him. In 1986 Vaughan went to a rehabilitation clinic in Atlanta and when he left it he was a new man. *In Step*, released in 1989, marked the beginning of a new and sober life and was also his greatest success to date: it gained 33rd place in the American charts and won a Grammy Award as the best blues album. That comeback was completed by March 1990 at which time Stevie went, with his brother Jimmy, to the studio to record the album *Family Style*. Unfortunately, the album was released posthumously. In August 1990, Double Trouble was invited to open Eric Clapton's two concerts at the Alpine Valley Music Theatre in East Troy, Wisconsin. The second evening, 26 August, ended with a spectacular jam session. Eric Clapton introduced Jimmy and Stevie on stage as "the two best guitarists in the world" before beginning to play with them in a very long version of *Sweet Home Chicago* that also included Robert Cray and Buddy Guy and created an electric atmosphere in the theatre. While backstage, Eric Clapton invited Stevie to play with him in a series of engagements at the Royal Albert Hall in London, but Stevie said he was very tired and wanted to go back to his hotel in Chicago. Eric Clapton offered his helicopter, a four-seat Bell 206 piloted by Jeff Brown. The tour manager Peter Jackson told Stevie that the helicopter had already been reserved for him, Jimmy and his wife Connie, and that the weather conditions were not the best so they had to take off very soon. When they arrived at the helicopter they found that the seats had already been occupied by three members of Eric Clapton's entourage, the bodyguard Nigel Browne, agent Bobby Brooks and the assistant Colin Smythe. Stevie asked his brother if he could take the last free seat, adding that he simply had to get back to Chicago. Jimmy agreed to take the next available helicopter. The Bell 206 took off in a thick fog and after only a few minutes crashed into a hill, killing all the passengers. The police report stated that although the pilot, Jeff Brown, had had a lot of experience, he was unable to see the hill because of the fog. Stevie Ray Vaughan was 35 years old. His brother Jimmy, together with others, wrote the song *Six Strings Down* as a tribute to him.

"GUITARIST STEVIE RAY VAUGHAN DIES IN WISCONSIN"

[Star Tribune]

178-179 Stevie Ray Vaughan and his band, Double Trouble. From left to right, bass guitarist Tommy Shannon and drummer Chris Leyton. The dramatic helicopter accident occurred after a memorable concert with Eric Clapton in Wisconsin, as the headline in the *Star Tribune* reports.

180 Stevie Ray Vaughan with his Fender Stratocaster. His favourite was a 1963 model he bought in 1974.

181 2 July 1987: Stevie Ray Vaughan performing live at the Community Center in Sacramento, California.

STEVE
CLARK

[23 April 1960 > 8 January 1991]

The story of Def Leppard consists of peaks and troughs. One of the pioneers of the New Wave of British Heavy Metal – which exploded onto the UK music scene in the late 1970s and also included the bands Iron Maiden, Motorhead and Judas Priest – Def Leppard became a pillar of commercial rock in the 1980s, especially in the United States. But, during the course of their long career, they had to overcome many obstacles, first among those being alcohol abuse and rehabilitation. Then there was the incredible motorway accident involving drummer Rick Allen in 1984 in which he lost his left arm. Two years later, at the Monsters of Rock festival held at Castle Donnington, Rick was greeted with an ovation while he sat behind a special electronic drum set that he could play with his feet and obtain the same results as he had formerly done with his two hands. He was the symbol of the indomitable spirit of Def Leppard.

The band was formed in Sheffield in 1977, when Rick Savage and Pete Willis, who played in a band called Atomic Mass, met Joe Elliott, a guitarist who was only 18 years old. Joe chose the name Deaf Leopard (later changed to Def Leppard), and although at first he wanted to play the guitar, he actually became the band's vocalist when it began to perform in Sheffield's rock pubs. The following year saw the arrival of drummer Rick Allen, who was only 15, and a new guitarist, Steve Clark.

The son of a taxi driver from the suburbs of Sheffield, Steve had played guitar since the age of 11. During his audition with Def Leppard he amazed everyone by playing Lynyrd Skynyrd's *Freebird* in its entirety. He became known as The Riffmaster, the man who, with Pete Willis, created the Def Leppard sound. But Steve also accompanied Pete in his alcohol problems. After the band's first two albums, *On Through the Night* (1980) and *High'n'Dry* (1981), Pete was removed from the band, because he drank too much, and was replaced by Phil Collen. With his guitar, Steve led Def Leppard to worldwide success with *Pyromania* (1983), which sold six million copies and *Hysteria (1987)* which topped the charts in both the UK and the US. The band had to wait three years to record *Hysteria* because of Rick Allen's terrible accident: instead of replacing him, the other members decided to wait for him to learn to play the drums again single-handed. After *Hysteria* they intended to waste no time to record their fifth album, *Adrenalize*, as soon as possible.

The problem was Steve Clark. His alcoholism was becoming worse and worse. The band tried to save him in every possible way. In 1989 Steve collapsed after a gig in Minneapolis and Def Leppard had him admitted to a rehab clinic. They then asked guitar technician Malvin Mortimer to watch Steve around the clock. But their attempts came to nothing and in August 1990 Steve had to take a six-month leave of absence from the band. His friends seemed to be resigned to the fact that nothing could help him any longer. On 7 January 1991 he spent the evening in a pub with his friend Daniel Van Alphen. The next day his girlfriend Janie Dean went to his home and found him lying dead on the sofa. Traces of Valium, codeine, morphine and alcohol were found in his system. The Riffmaster was only 30. Six of the songs in Def Leppard's new album had his signature.

DEAD

[16 January 1969 > 8 April 1991]

EURONYMOUS

[22 March 1968 > 10 August 1993]

This account describes one of the most disturbing episodes in rock. If there is a metal music Hell, it is in Norway. It is the story of the band Mayhem, a major originator of Norwegian black metal music with its distressing records, violent performances, Satanism and madness, a band that ended up destroying itself through acts of murder and suicide.

Mayhem was founded in 1984 by the guitarist Oystein Aarseth, better known by his stage name "Euronymous," and released its debut album, *Deathcrush*, in 1987. That had been a stand taken against the other Nordic metal bands which, according to Euronymous had been "guilty" of not having promoted, vigorously, the cult of death. The 1,000 copy run of *Deathcrush* sold out quickly in Norway and launched the band, which in 1988 changed its line-up with the arrival of drummer Jan Axel Blomberg (stage name "Hellhammer") and vocalist Per Yngve Ohlin, a dark figure who chose the stage name "Dead." And, in fact, he was a person who had always played with death. As a boy he had been beaten at school, by bullies, which had caused internal bleeding that almost killed him. Since that time he always claimed that he was already dead. He painted his face black and white and buried his clothes before wearing them in order to look, and smell, like a corpse. He also declared that blood no longer flowed in his veins and when he asked to be auditioned by Mayhem he sent them a crucified mouse with his demo. Dead felt that he did not belong to this world and was

viewed with fear even by the other members of Mayhem. But his extreme interpretation of the aesthetic canons of black metal music contributed to the band's success. It also triggered violent acts on the part of its fans. The Norwegian press began to write about churches being attacked and of something strange that was developing among the young people of the country. Black metal became a fad and conquered Norway. In 1990 Mayhem took up residence in an old house, in the forests outside Oslo, to work on their album *De Mysteriis Dom Sathanas* (1994) which is considered to be a manifesto of the black metal genre. The lyrics were almost all morbid compositions written by Dead, during and after 1987, but his career ended a short time before it really began. On 6 April 1991 the boy who wanted to die committed suicide in the band's house. He cut his veins and throat and then shot himself in the head, leaving a message: "Excuse all the blood, cheers." It was an absurd act that left his work unfinished and that created even more disturbing legends. The first person to find Dead's body was Euronymous, who, instead of immediately calling the police, ran to the nearest store, bought a camera and took photos of the corpse, one of which was used on the cover of a bootleg live album *Dawn of the Black Hearts* (1995). It was rumoured that he had also cooked and eaten pieces of his friend's brain and that fragments of his skull were converted into jewels that the band members wore and also distributed to other black metal bands to honour his memory.

In order to complete the recording of the album Euronymous found a new vocalist, the Hungarian Attila Csihar, and a bass guitarist, Kristian Varg Vikernes (stage name "Count Grishnackh") who also played in his own one-man band, Burzum. But the album had not yet been released because the madness continued. Varg Vikernes had already been arrested and charged with having planned to burn down a church, and he made a plan, with Euronymous, to blow up Trondheim's Nidaros Cathedral, a photograph of which was on the album cover. The two seemed to get along famously, at least until 1993. On 10 August Varg Vikernes drove about 310 miles from Bergen to Euronymous' home in Oslo. He wanted to clarify matters concerning the Burzum recording project and he was not happy with the management of Deathlike Silence Productions, the Oslo-based independent record label. And, perhaps, there were other motives that brought about a violent argument between the two. Varg pulled a knife and stabbed Euronymous 23 times. When questioned by the police, he claimed that he had acted merely out of self-defence and that the many wounds had been caused by the broken glass that Euronymous had fallen on during their fight. He was sentenced to 21 years imprisonment. The police found over 300 pounds of explosives in his house. The Norwegian Hell had claimed its victims. Upon release, *De Mysteriis Dom Sathanas* still contained Dead's lyrics, the bass parts of Varg Vikernes and Euronymous' guitar playing.

185 Dead and Euronymous on the cover of the bootleg album *A Tribute to Black Emperors* released by Mayhem in 1997. In an interview, Euronymous stated that his friend had committed suicide because he could not tolerate the trivial public and the spread of black metal bands he considered phony and commercial.

"DEAD WAS BORED WITH ALL THE WIMPS, TRENDIES AND FALSE BLACK METAL SITES IN THE WORLD SO HE DECIDED TO END HIS EARTHLY LIFE"

[Euronymous]

A TRIBUTE TO THE BLACK EMPERORS

JOHNNY THUNDERS

[15 July 1952 > 23 April 1991]

In 1991 Johnny Thunders was a kind of fossil, a former glory of rock music afflicted with the typical problems caused by a life of excess. His story was that of a generation of street urchins from Queens, New York who, in the early 1970s, created and lived the punk lifestyle, with all the risks that entailed. His musical career began in 1967 under the name Johnny Volume (his real name was John Anthony Genzale Jr.) in Johnny and the Jaywalkers. In subsequent years Johnny often went to Nobody's, a club on Bleecker Street, where he met Arthur Kane and Rick Rivets and joined their band, Actress. In 1971 three others joined the band – Sylvain Sylvain (who replaced Rick Rivets), Billy Murcia and David Johansen – which changed its name to the New York Dolls. Their first concert was on Christmas night, 1971, at the Endicott Hotel, a former luxury establishment that, in the 1960s, had become a homeless shelter and a refuge for criminals and drug addicts. The hotel employees offered the band a gig in exchange for a free supper. That was the beginning of the story of one of the most decadent bands of the 1970s, which created a form of hard rock that anticipated both punk and heavy metal. The New York Dolls played just about everywhere in New York, from the Mercer Arts Center to the transvestite haunt, Club 82, in the East Village. They became a cult band but scared away the record labels which refused to engage them because of their transgressive and vulgar lifestyle. In 1972 the band began to pay dearly for their excesses: during their first UK tour, drummer Billy Murcia drowned, before he had even recorded with the band. He was only 21. In 1973 Jerry Nolan replaced Murcia and the New York Dolls released their debut album, *New York Dolls*, which reached only number 116 in the American charts.

The band divided and upset people. In 1973 a poll organised by *Creem* magazine they were elected the best and worst band of the year. The following year the band chose George Morton as their producer – famous for having launched the Shangri-Las and other female groups in the 1960s. The result was *Too Much Too Soon*, which peaked even lower in the charts. Their last attempt at success was entrusted to Malcolm McLaren, who experimented with his ability in transforming shock into publicity. But, while that trick had worked with the Sex Pistols, it failed with the New York Dolls: McLaren had the band members wear red leather outfits and play in front of a huge Soviet Union flag during a mini tour of five concerts in the five boroughs of New York City while accompanied by a new band, Television. At that point Thunders decided to leave the New York Dolls. Their first two albums remain among the most important cult records in the history of rock, the testimony of a band devoted to self-destruction.

In 1975 Johnny formed The Heartbreakers with Jerry Nolan, Walter Lure and Richard Hell (who left the band a few months later and was replaced by Billy Rath). That marked the beginning of a new career, which proved to be even more transgressive than the one with the Dolls. On 1 December 1976 The Heartbreakers landed in London with only a one-way ticket in their hands and without a work permit, bringing along a dangerous addiction to heroin and a groupie who was also a junkie, Nancy Spungen. That was the Anarchy Tour, a series of concerts performed with the Clash, the Sex Pistols and the Damned that helped to make punk popular throughout the UK but which, according to many people, led to the ruin of many bands on the English since they were too young and ingenuous to cope with the heroin consumption typical of The Heartbreakers and the mad behaviour of Nancy Spungen, who went to London to follow Jerry Nolan and found Sid Vicious instead. The Heartbreakers stayed in the UK for the whole of 1977, recorded their only album, *L.A.M.F.*, made another tour and then split up due to their excesses and internal rivalry and disputes. Johnny stayed in London and recorded *So Alone* and also organised a series of concerts at the Speakeasy club, with the name Johnny Thunders Rebels and The Living Dead, with the participation of many musicians, such as former Sex Pistols Sid Vicious, Steve Jones and Paul Cook, Phil Lynott of Thin Lizzy, Steve Marriott of Small Faces and Chrissie Hynde of the Pretenders. After *So Alone*, Johnny seemed to want to stop his reckless life, stating he had returned to

188 and 189 Johnny Thunders with the New York Dolls. The make-up and attire anticipated the glam period but, musically speaking, the band created a new form of hard rock that paved the way for punk and heavy metal. Thunders said: "The Dolls were an attitude. If nothing else they were a great attitude."

the United States, got married and had children. But then he moved to Detroit and met Wayne Kramer of MC5 and formed Gang War. His attempt to lead a peaceful, normal life with his wife Julie did not last long. In 1979 Johnny returned to the stage with Gang War, but two years later he was penniless in New York. He somehow always managed to get his act together again and resurface. In 1982 he resumed his rock 'n' roll trips, often playing in London (where he was arrested for drug possession) with his friends on the British punk scene. He celebrated his 30th birthday with a concert at the Irving Plaza in New York, then flew to Sweden with his new girlfriend Susanne Blomqvist and reunited The Heartbreakers for a series of tours of Europe and Japan. In subsequent years he continued to perform. He had no house and was unable to create a stable life with Susanne. He travelled and performed continuously in Scandinavia, the UK and the United States, always changing his band (one of the last was with Jerry Nolan and Glen Matlock of the Sex Pistols). The only recordings he made during that time were *Que Sera Sera* and *Copy Cats*, a collection of covers recorded with Patti Palladin.

His adventures and excesses became legendary. A physician in London prescribed a methadone therapy to cure his heroin dependence and in the following years Johnny flew to the UK every two months for medical visits. The last four months of his life were an unbridled race: in 1991 Johnny played in Paris and in Japan with his new band then went to Thailand passed through London and flew to Germany to record his last song, a cover of *Born to Lose* with Die Toten Hosen. On 22 April he arrived in New Orleans and registered in room 37 of the St. Peter Guest House. He was 38 and was seriously attempting to break his heroin habit. But he was also concealing a secret: he had leukaemia. On 23 April 1991 he was found dead, lying in the foetal position under a table. The police immediately closed the case, stating that Johnny had died of an overdose. He was only one of the many addicts who had gone to New Orleans to die. But his demise immediately took on mysterious implications. According to his biographer Nina Antonia, the level of drugs in his blood was not high enough to cause his death. Furthermore, Johnny's passport, clothes and wallet were missing. His friends claimed someone had killed him in order to steal his large supply of methadone. The police never reopened the case. Singer Willy De Ville, who stayed in the room next to his, told the press that Johnny Thunders had died with his guitar in his hands, a lie obviously invented as a sign of respect. But one thing is certain: few other musicians lived a rock 'n' roll life like Johnny Thunders.

FREDDIE
MERCURY

[5 September 1946 > 24 November 1991]

"The most important thing, darling, is to live a fabulous life. As long as it's fabulous, I don't care how long it is." Freddie Mercury was the symbol of the extravagant creativity of Queen and an overwhelming, global rock star who always represented the spirit of his time during his 20-year career. Freddie Mercury lived in the London of the late 1960s spirit, made his debut in the glam era and represented the apex of virtuosity in the early 1970s, when he wrote his masterpiece, *Bohemian Rhapsody*. He then led Queen into hard rock in the mid-1970s and pop in the 1980s, working with electronic sound, video clips and experimenting with his personal research into a fusion of all art forms that projected him into uncharted territory. And, with his matchless gifts as a lead singer, he made Queen one of the greatest live bands in the history of rock, while living his life to the limit. Once asked whether he enjoyed fame, he replied: "I know nothing else. To me it's normal. It's like winning the pools every day."

Freddie Mercury loved to amaze people, to sing and enjoy himself; he loved being the top star in the world. And he paid too high a price for his will to live: "If I didn't do this well, I just wouldn't have anything to do...I can't cook, and I'd be a terrible housewife. I want to keep on having success, writing beautiful songs and falling in love." Freddie Mercury was diagnosed HIV positive in 1987. He decided to face his illness by continuing to work right to the end. He spent his final years between his Garden Lodge house in Kensington, London and his villa in

Montreux with a view of the lake, just a few steps away from Queen's Mountain Studios where they recorded their last two albums, *The Miracle* and *Innuendo*, as well as the songs on the posthumous album *Made in Heaven*. He kept close to his inner circle of trusted friends: stylist Diana Mosley, his personal assistants Peter Freestone and Joe Fanelli, his first love Mary Austin and his partner Jim Hutton. Freddie had openly told each of them that they had to be prepared to accept the worst and that afterwards they had to continue to live as they had always done. Freddie Mercury remained true to himself to the end, with his extravagant and grandiose lifestyle. He bought another apartment, in Montreux, and carefully chose the furnishings despite the fact that he knew very well that he would never live there. Peter Freestone recalled later that he had been resigned to the fact that he was about to die and had accepted it, adding that it would have been difficult to imagine an aged Freddie Mercury. At Montreux, a place that in normal conditions might have been terribly boring, Freddie had found the serenity that he had sought all his life and wrote his final two songs, *A Winter's Tale* and *Mother Love,* which would be the final portrait of a poetic soul clinging, melancholically but fearlessly, to a life that was vanishing minute by minute. In his London home he resumed drawing, something he had not done since he had attended Ealing Art College, and did abstract watercolours as well as portraits of his cats. He made his exit in a grandiose and unpredictable manner, just as he

had always lived: the last Queen single was *The Show Must Go On*, while his final appearance was in the music video *These Are the Days of Our Lives*, where he seemed to be fragile and ethereal, almost on the verge of disappearing. He had recorded his parts alone but did not fail to appear in the last scene in order to whisper "I still love you" to his public. And then he disappeared with a typical theatrical gesture. On 23 November 1991 he issued the following announcement: "Following the enormous conjecture in the press over the last two weeks, I wish to confirm that I have been tested HIV positive and have AIDS. I felt it correct to keep this information private to date to protect the privacy of those around me. However, the time has come now for my friends and fans around the world to know the truth and I hope that everyone will join with me, my doctors, and all those worldwide in the fight against this terrible disease. My privacy has always been very special to me and I am famous for my lack of interviews. Please understand this policy will continue."

The next day at 7.00 pm, Sunday 24 November 1991, Freddie Mercury died of a sudden attack of bronchial pneumonia. He was just 45. His body was cremated on 27 November in London after a private ceremony attended by his family and a few friends, including Elton John. The funeral service was conducted in keeping with the precepts of Zoroastrianism, the religion of his parents. The music played during the ceremony was Aretha Franklin's version of *You've Got a Friend* and the aria of Verdi's

Showman . . . Freddie draped in a Union Flag during a typically flamboyant performance

THE Sun
FREDDIE IS DEAD

Monday, November 25, 1991 25p Audited daily sale for October 3,705,400 Today's TV: Pages 16 and 17

1946   1991

By BARRIE WATTS

ROCK star Freddie Mercury is dead — just two days after confirming he had AIDS.

The 45-year-old gay star's parents were at his bedside as he slipped away late last night.

Freddie's doctor and close friend Gordon Atkinson was also with the Queen singer at his £4million mansion.

Dr Atkinson made three signed statements to the house in Kensington, West London, where he died, on the actual cause of death.

Freddie Mercury died peacefully this evening at his home from broncho-pneumonia, brought on by AIDS."

Showman was revealed after Freddie announced on Saturday that he had the killer virus. DJ Tony Blackburn, who has lived next door to him for two years, said: "Freddie was a bit of a recluse."

Just before midnight, the star's spokesman Roxy Meade said: "Freddie Mercury died peacefully this evening at his home from broncho-pneumonia, brought on by AIDS."

Continued on Page Four

175 top Freddie Mercury on stage with Queen during their *Live Killers* tour.

175 bottom 25 November 1991: the front page of *The Sun* announces the death of Freddie Mercury.

Il Trovatore, D'amor sull ali rosee, sung by Montserrat Caballé. Freddie left a good portion of his estate to the fight against AIDS, especially the Terence Higgins Trust. Queen released a single with *Bohemian Rhapsody* and *These Are the Days of Our Lives* that sold 100,000 copies in a week, immediately went to number one in the charts and the proceeds of which amounted to over one million pounds.

The whereabouts of his ashes are believed to be known only to Mary Austin. There is no tomb or monument to Freddie in the UK. On his birthday and on the anniversary of his death fans gather in front of his former home, Garden Lodge, where Mary Austin now lives. The only monument to Mercury has been that sculpted by Irena Sedlecka; it is situated in Montreux, on the shore of Lake Geneva. At the end of 1991, Queen made an official statement: "We have lost the greatest and most beloved member of our family. We feel overwhelming grief that he has gone, sadness that he should be cut down at the height of his creativity, but above all great pride in the courageous way he loved and died. It has been a privilege for us to have shared such magical times. As soon as we are able we would like to celebrate his life in the style to which he was accustomed." This desire was realised with one of the most impressive events of the 1990s, the Freddie Mercury Tribute concert at Wembley Stadium. Brian May, Roger Taylor and John Deacon had personally contacted various musicians and bands and on 27 March 1992 they got together, to play for the first time without Freddie, in a studio in Shepherd's Bush in London, after which they moved to the Bray Studios in Berkshire to wait for their guests. The guest list was quite impressive: David Bowie, Annie Lennox, Guns N' Roses, Metallica, Extreme, Def Leppard, Elton John, George Michael, Robert Plant, Mick Ronson, Tony Iommi, Ian Hunter, Bob Geldof, Seal, Lisa Stansfield, Paul Young, Zucchero and Liza Minnelli. On 20 April 1992 the stars of international rock and pop were at Wembley Stadium to celebrate the art and life of Freddie Mercury. There were 100,000 people present, all with their eyes riveted to the huge stage, which was surmounted by a 42 feet high phoenix. After more than 7 hours of music, the lights went out on an event that had been viewed on TV by more than one billion viewers worldwide. In a letter to the Queen fan club, Brian May wrote the following testimonial: "Music and his friends were everything to Freddie, and he devoted himself body and soul to them. Freddie, his music, his amazing creative energy, all this will never die." But the definitive words concerning his incredible career came from Freddie Mercury himself: "If I had to do this all over again, yes why not, I'd do it slightly differently."

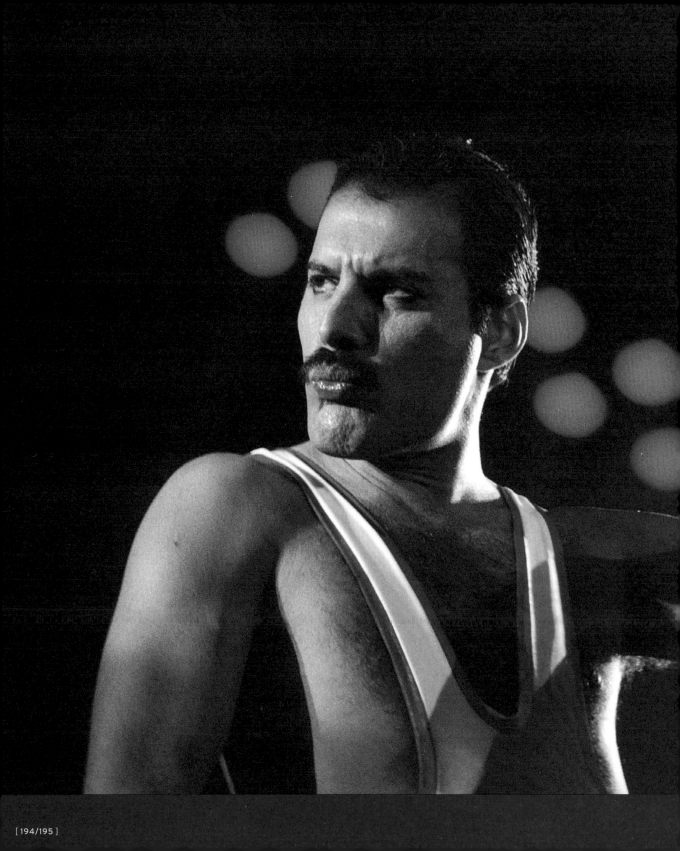

DAILY Star

BRITAIN'S BRIGHTEST NEWSPAPER

MONDAY, NOVEMBER 25, 1991 — Only 25p ...

FREDDIE MERCURY: LAST TRAGIC HOURS

AIDS KILLS THE KING OF ROCK

Music world is in mourning for Queen's superstar singer

FREDDIE'S NIGHTMARE Pages 2-3

DEATH OF A SUPERSTAR: The final curtain for pop's brilliant but tragic Freddie

TRAGIC rock star Freddie Mercury finally lost his agonising two-year battle against AIDS last night.

He died at his £4 million London home a gaunt shadow of the flamboyant singer who had taken the pop world by storm.

Freddie, 45, had confessed at the weekend that the years of one-night stands had caught up with him — and that he was HIV positive.

The final curtain was one the Queen singer had long feared. He was a self-confessed bi-sexual and three of his former gay lovers had died of AIDS.

It was a lonely end for Freddie, who always claimed to be one of the loneliest men in the world. The whole rock world was in mourning last night over the loss of a true superstar.

194 Freddie Mercury photographed in 1984 during *The Works* tour. He once said: "The reason we're successful, darling? My overall charisma, of course."

195 top 25 November 1991: the front page of the *Daily Star* announces the death of the rock star due to AIDS.

195 bottom 27 November 1991: Elton John and Brian May at Freddie Mercury's funeral.

197 The void created by the absence of the Queen's frontman, with his overwhelming personality, could never be filled. *The Independent* was well aware of this when it asked who would ever dare wear Freddie Mercury's crown.

"WHO DARES WEAR FREDDIE MERCURY'S CROWN?"

[The Independent]

KURT COBAIN

"I wish there was someone I could ask for advice, someone who wouldn't make me feel like a creep for spilling my guts and trying to explain all the insecurities that have plagued me for oh, about 25 years now." Kurt Cobain's soul can be read in his diaries, hundreds of hand-written pages in spiral notebooks, hotel note pads and even restaurant menus. His thoughts written down while on tour are like photographs of confused and disorderly moods, yet they are lucid in their description of a different sensitivity that could not identify with a difficult and incomprehensible world. It had always been that way for him.

Kurt was born in Aberdeen, Washington, a place he called a ghetto for lumberjacks dominated by a lack of culture. He never felt accepted; not by his parents, who divorced when he was seven years old, not by his school friends who taunted him because he had a gay friend, not by society, which wanted him to be "normal." His aunt gave him his first guitar together with the first three Beatles records and then his encounter with punk and classical rock led him towards an alternative style and approach. He loved to play, to go to concerts, to write and to paint. But his friendship with Buzz Osborne and Dale Crover of the Melvins triggered his decision to be a musician. Punk rock meant freedom for him, a way to forget Aberdeen. He left school only a few weeks before graduating and his mother

threw him out of the house. He tried to find a job and became a roadie for the Melvins. In 1985 he formed his own band, Nirvana, with Krist Novoselic, another devotee of punk rock whom Kurt had met in the Melvins' rehearsal hall. They tried out various drummers and finally chose Chad Channing. Nirvana debuted with *Bleach*, a raw and raucous album recorded in only 40 hours in 1989 and released by Sub Pop Records, the independent label that launched the Seattle scene. The title refers to an American Aids prevention poster that invited drug users to sterilise their needles with bleach. Kurt decided that this was the substance that would save humanity. "I tried heroin the first time in 1987 in Aberdeen," Kurt wrote in his diaries. "[...] When I got back from our second European Tour with Sonic Youth I decided to use heroin on a daily basis because an ongoing stomach ailment that I had been suffering from for the past five years had literally taken me to the point of wanting to kill myself. [...] So I decided I feel like a junky as it is so I may as well be one."

In April 1990 Nirvana began work on their second album with producer Butch Vig at Smart Studios in Madison, Wisconsin. In the meantime things had changed. Nirvana left Sub Pop Records and signed with a major label, Geffen Records, which had them use Sound City Studios in Van Nuys, California. Chad Channing was no longer the drummer, having been replaced by Dave Grohl

who lent power and precision to the band, while the arrangements made the harsh, angry Nirvana sound more engrossing. That was the sound of *Nevermind*, an album of truly hard-core punk rock that immediately seized an entire generation, which considered it a mainstream pop album, thus changing the 1990s' idea of music. *Nevermind* was released on 24 September 1991 and sold 400,000 copies in only two weeks. In January 1992 it topped the American Billboard charts, replacing Michael Jackson's *Dangerous*. The famous album cover is an open declaration of opposition to the materialism of modern society, as well as a form of self-irony, since the band had suddenly decided to leave the independent circuit. Cobain said that he had thought a lot about *Nevermind*'s success without reaching a conclusion and considered it better than most of the trash produced at the time. In a period dominated by commercial products, Nirvana announced a return to the purity and abrasive quality of rock consisting of simple, rough chords and a sincere voice, the concept of music as authentic expression and a sublimation of pain and anguish.

But for Kurt Cobain that was not to be the case. Success is a machine that can destroy one. He was not prepared to have his privacy invaded by millions of curious people and to always feel out of place: "I have been forced to become a reclusive rock star." The critics viewed Nirvana

199 Kurt Cobain formed Nirvana with Krist Novoselic in 1987 in Aberdeen, Washington. In 1989 they released their first album, *Bleach*, which was followed by *Nevermind* (1991) and *In Utero* (1993). *Nevermind* has sold more than 30 million copies.

200-201 September 1990: Kurt Cobain at Krist Novoselic's home in Seattle.

201 June 1989. The first Nirvana line-up: Kurt Cobain, Dan Peters, Chad Channing and Krist Novoselic.

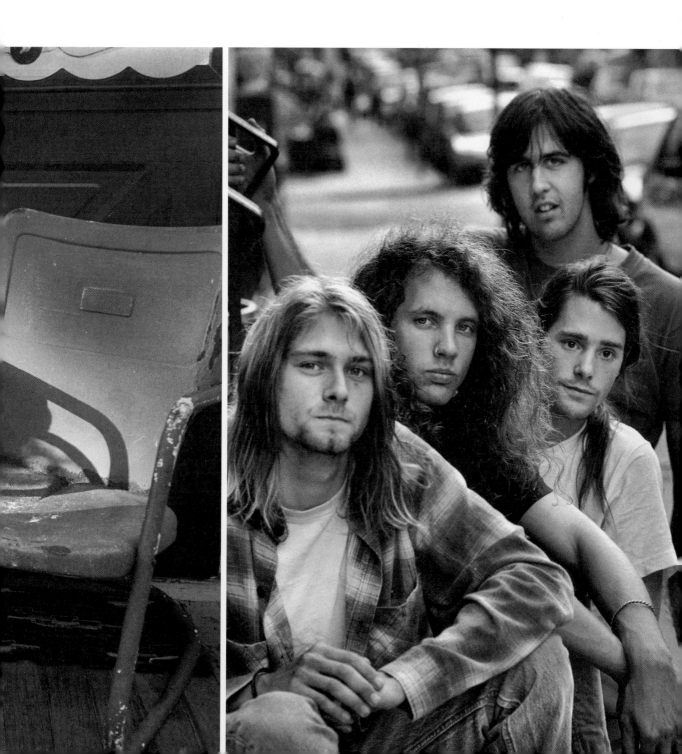

202-203 Kurt Cobain during the *Unplugged* concert recorded for MTV at the Sony Music Studios in New York on 18 November 1993. The album *MTV Unplugged in New York* was released on 1 November 1994, seven months after Cobain's death. It topped the American charts and sold 5 million copies.

203 top An historic photograph of Kurt Cobain's corpse taken by Tom Reese for the *Seattle Times*.

songs as the portrait of a disturbed generation that has no ideals, holds little hope and is threatened by depression. But Cobain claimed he never wanted to impart any real sense to his lyrics, which he considered "a big pile of contradictions." For him his music was not, nor did it intend to be, the symbol of his generation. It was simply a part of it. He had merely set to music the screams of thousands of youngsters like himself, expressing a personal angst that was shared by others and was, therefore, universal. "I'm a spokesman for myself," he said. "It just so happens that there's a bunch of people that are concerned with what I have to say. I find that frightening at times because I'm just as confused as most people." The success of *Nevermind* marked the beginning of his end. Kurt was trapped in the show business mechanism. He felt he was a pure artist forced to sell out, he felt used and abused. One of the songs on Nirvana's third album, *In Utero*, is entitled *Rape Me*. The band recorded the album in only two weeks in a remote studio in Cannon Falls, Minnesota with Steve Albini, the producer of *Surfer Rosa*, a fundamental album of Cobain's favourite band, the Pixies. The album became a sort of handbook for the indie music spirit performed by a band of superstars. Nirvana paid for the recording sessions out of their own pockets and did not tell the managers of Geffen Records about the album until everything was finished. Kurt also wanted to give it a devastating title: *I Hate Myself and I Want to Die*.

In Utero was released on 13 September 1993. Cobain said: "We're certain that we won't sell a quarter as much, and we're totally comfortable with that because we like this record so much." But in fact it entered the charts at number one and sold five million copies. The success machine leaves no way of escape. Cobain could no longer endure the contradiction of continuing to produce music that stemmed from his deepest inner feelings, only to see it become a mass product. Nirvana played for the last time on 1 March 1994, in Munich. Four days later, at the Hotel Excelsior in Rome, Kurt fell into a coma due to a combination of Rohypnol and champagne. Was that an accident or attempted suicide? There was nothing left to keep him anchored to life, not even his daughter Francis Bean, born to his wife Courtney Love. Theirs was a turbulent relationship that was analysed to the Nth degree by the media and that had by then become violent and more and more painful. On 25 March 1994, Courtney and her boyfriend Dylan Carlson persuaded Kurt to begin a detox program. On 30 March Kurt went to the Exodus Recovery Center in Los Angeles, but stayed there for only two days. He ran away and took a plane to Seattle. Then he disappeared. Courtney hired a private detective to find out where he was. He had gone to his villa at 171 Lake Washington Boulevard East, an upper-class neighbourhood on the outskirts of Seattle, where he hid in the greenhouse above the garage and where he shot himself in the head with a Remington M-11 rifle.

He was found on the morning of 8 April 1994 by an electrician who had gone there to fix the alarm system. The coroner stated that Cobain had been dead for three days. Next to his body was a note addressed to his childhood imaginary friend, Boddah, which was the final brushstroke on the portrait of a disturbed soul. Kurt wrote that he had not felt enthusiastic about listening to and writing music for many years. He also felt guilty and didn't want to deceive his fans any longer and make them believe he was enjoying himself: "I have it good, very good, and I'm grateful, but since the age of seven, I've become hateful towards all humans in general. Only because it seems so easy for people to get along and have empathy. Only because I love and feel sorry for people too much I guess. Thank you all from the pit of my burning, nauseous stomach for your letters and concern during the past years. I'm too much of an erratic, moody baby! I don't have the passion anymore, and so remember, it's better to burn out than to fade away."

205 "I like to dream that someday we will have the sense of generational solidarity amongst the youth of the world. I like to make insidious strong options with nothing to back them up with besides my primary sincerity. I like sincerity. I lack sincerity. These are not words of wisdom, this is a disclaimer for my lack of education, for my loss of inspiration, for my unnerving quest for affection and my perfunctory shamefulness towards many who are of my relative age. It's not even a poem. It's just a big pile of shit. Like me." Kurt Cobain.

SHANNON
HOON

[26 September 1967 > 21 October 1995]

Richard Shannon Hoon wrote his first song, *Change*, in 1985, when he was only 18 years old: "And when you feel your life ain't worth living / You've got to stand up and take a look around you / Then a look way up to the sky. [...] When life is hard, you have to change." Shannon Hoon was an Indiana boy who sang in a band called Styff Kytten. Since her school days his sister, Anna, had been a friend of Axl Rose, the singer with Guns N' Roses. It was that song and that friendship that launched Shannon's career in rock music. In 1989 Shannon Hoon moved to Los Angeles and one night, while he was playing *Change* at a party, he met two other musicians, Brad Smith and Rogers Stevens, who asked him to play with them. That was the birth of Blind Melon, one the most promising bands in 1990s indie rock music.

In the meantime, Shannon had befriended Axl Rose, who invited him to the studio during the recording of the twin Guns N' Roses albums, *Use Your Illusion I* and *II*. Shannon accompanied Rose on some of the songs and also appeared in the video clip *Don't Cry*, which became one of the most popular singles that year.

The stage was set for Blind Melon to become the new sensation of American indie rock music. However, there was a problem: Shannon Hoon was dangerously addicted to drugs. He would mix hallucinogens and marijuana to follow his psychedelic inspiration but he also used heroin and cocaine. And success seemed to aggravate his problems. In 1992 Blind Melon moved to a house in Durham, North Carolina and recorded their first self-titled album, the opening track of which, *No Rain*, narrates a surreal story of solitude and redemption that fascinated the

Generation X public and took the album *Blind Melon* to the number three spot in the American charts. After the release the band immediately went on tour for almost two years. And Shannon became ungovernable. During a concert in October 1993 in Orlando, when he was a support for Lenny Kravitz's act, he went onstage smoking marijuana and in Vancouver he was arrested for urinating on a member of the audience. In 1994 he ended the Woodstock show totally zonked on acid and threw a piece of the drum set into the audience. That same year, during the Billboard Music Awards, he assaulted one of the security guards.

Arrests, excess, mayhem – Hoon followed the path of a psychedelic rock star lifestyle and seemed unable to stop. At least until July 1995 when his daughter Nico Blue was born. Blind Melon was about to release its second album, *Soup*, and Shannon decided to quit drugs. He followed a rehabilitation program and when he had finished he hired a personal drug counsellor to stay with him day and night. It looked as if he would manage to kick his drug habit. But the band had to make a tour to promote *Soup*. The counsellor was dead set against it but the band went off anyway. And Shannon's career ended at the age of 28, in the morning of 21 October 1995, in New Orleans. Blind Melon had scheduled a date at Tipitina's Club. A roadie went into the band's tour bus to wake Shannon up in time for the sound check. But Shannon did not wake up. He had died of an accidental overdose of cocaine. His drug counsellor had been fired a few days earlier.

The boy from Indiana lies at rest in a Dayton cemetery. Carved on his tomb are the verses of his first song, *Change*.

"SHANNON HOON DIED ON SATURDAY IN THE BAND'S TOUR BUS IN A PARKING LOT IN NEW ORLEANS."

[The New York Times]

JEFF BUCKLEY

The year 1994 witnessed the release of an album, *Grace*, that immediately became an integral part of the history of rock music. It marked the amazing debut of an extremely handsome and restless singer, Jeff Buckley.

Jeff Buckley's story is one of those that makes one think that, in the world of rock music, something called destiny really exists and that when art is pure it can consume someone's existence. Jeff Buckley was the son of Tim Buckley, a gifted singer in the 1900s who had had an incredible voice that ranged from folk via psychedelia to jazz. Tim Buckley had died in 1975 when only 28 years old, devastated by a life of excess and unremitting anxiety. His voice and his talent were passed on to his son Jeff who, in his brief life, seemed to bear a curse. At the age of eight, Jeff had met his father for the first time, in the spring of 1975. Tim had not been present at his son's birth on 17 November 1966 in Anaheim, California. He had abandoned his wife, Mary Guibert, a few months earlier to pursue a career as a musician. So Jeff grew up in Orange County with his mother and her new partner, Ron Moorhead. Shortly after he met his son, Tim Buckley had died of a drug overdose.

Jeff Buckley got his first guitar, a Gibson Les Paul, when he was 13. He decided that he wanted to become a musician. He was obsessed by his father's heritage. His debut as a singer came about on 26 April 1991 in St. Ann's Church in Brooklyn, the same church in which Lou Reed and John Cale had played in memory of Andy Warhol,

in 1989. That had been a truly special occasion for Jeff, an evening dedicated to the memory of his father. Accompanied by his guitarist Gary Lucas, Jeff went onstage and sang a song that his father had written, for him and his mother, *I Never Asked To Be Your Mountain*. The audience had been overwhelmed by the revelation of such pure talent: "It bothered me that I hadn't been to his funeral, that I'd never been able to tell him anything," Jeff had said. "I used that show to pay my last respects." Indeed, the concert served to exorcise the ghost of his relationship with his father and also helped launch his own career. In 1993 Jeff Buckley made his debut with the live EP *Live at Sin-é*, which had been recorded during one of his shows at the *Sin-é* café in St. Mark's Place, New York. It contained only four songs, but they had been enough to amaze the world with his voice, especially the song *Eternal Life* and a 10-minute cover of Van Morrison's *The Way Young Lovers Do*. A year later, Jeff Buckley had released his first album, *Grace*, consisting of ten songs of pure poetry that were to prove a pivotal work in the history of 1990s rock music.

There was a mystical aura about Jeff Buckley, he had an angelic voice and conquered the public with his charisma and his fragile and romantic spirit. But he was restless and anxiety-ridden. He had made a long, triumphal, world tour, but had not been able to put together a new album and, what is more, had had problems with his band. In 1996 he began work on an album, *My Sweetheart The Drunk*, with Tom Verlaine

from the band Television, but had not been pleased with the sessions.

He decided to move to Memphis, Tennessee and make a fresh start. Every evening he played at Barrister's, a bar in downtown Memphis, where he tried out new songs that he had recorded himself as demos using a using four track deck. Finally satisfied, he asked his band and the producer of *Grace*, Andy Wallace, to come to Memphis to finish the album. The recording sessions were due to begin on 30 May 1997. But fate was lying in wait for Jeff Buckley. The evening of 29 May 1997 he was with a friend, Keith Foti, at Wolf River Harbor, a slackwater channel of the Mississippi. They had been driving around and Jeff said that he wanted to take a walk along the riverside. They had a guitar and a portable radio with them. At 9.00 pm Jeff suddenly decided to go for a swim. Keith watched him dive into the water. He had been fully dressed and had been singing the chorus of the Led Zeppelin's *Whole Lotta Love*. A boat passed by and left a wake. Keith moved the radio and the guitar so that they wouldn't get wet. When he looked up to find Jeff, he couldn't see him any longer. The river had swallowed him up. His body was found a few days later, on 4 June 1997, in the Mississippi. An autopsy revealed that Jeff Buckley, age 30, had drowned. There had been no trace of either alcohol or drugs in his body. It had been a purely accidental death. A curse.

"Well it's my time coming," he'd sung on *Grace*, "I'm not afraid to die. My fading voice sings of love..."

211 An intense portrait of Jeff Buckley, who once declared: "If I didn't make music I would be completely insane. Or [...] I'd take up something else. Anything artistic. But music seems to me to be the most closely identified with my soul."

MICHAEL HUTCHENCE

[22 January 1960 > 22 November 1997]

Suicide Blonde was the song that epitomised the wild, desperate life of Michael Hutchence, vocalist and songwriter of INXS. The Suicide Blonde was Paula Yates, the beautiful TV presenter who, like him, was damned and who, in 1985, interviewed him on *The Tube*. In 1985 INXS was at a turning point in its career. The band was formed in 1977, in Sydney, Australia as The Farriss Brothers.

INXS began playing in the rock pubs of Sydney and then, in 1980, cut their debut *INXS*. *Underneath the Colours*, released in 1981, marked their first home success, while the following album, *Shabooh Shoobah*, paved the way for US success. Three years later the band created a sensation with *Kick*, which went to number three in the US charts and sold ten million copies and included their greatest hit, *Need You Tonight*. Hutchence became a super star and got engaged to Kylie Minogue. INXS did not record any albums for three years, until they released *X*, which went to number two in the UK charts and number five in the US, and which included *Suicide Blonde*. According to Michael Hutchence himself, inspiration for this song came from Kylie Minogue, who dyed her hair platinum blonde for a movie role. But the Suicide Blonde had already become a part of his life. There was still time for a relationship with model Helena Christensen and for an episode that would greatly influence his life. While he was leaving a club in Copenhagen, with Helena Christensen they had a collision with a taxi. He and the driver got into a row and Michael fell to the ground and fractured his skull. The result was a loss of his sense of smell and a

partial loss of his sense of taste. Many friends and acquaintances stated that that was what led to his bouts of depression and increasingly violent behaviour. During the recording sessions for *Full Moon, Dirty Hearts* (1993), Michael threatened bass guitarist Gary Beers with a knife. Movie director Richard Lowenstein told how Michael once wept in his arms, saying: "I can't smell or taste my girlfriend!"

It is said that the sense of smell is deeply connected to our emotions, that it is what creates the very fabric of life. In 1994 Michael was invited to take part in Paula Yates' provocative new TV show, *Big Breakfast*. The two fell in love instantly. Paula was still married to Bob Geldof and they had three daughters. She separated from her husband in 1995, which led to a long legal battle over custody of the children. Naturally, her relationship with Michael interested the press, eager to exploit the love triangle. The pressure and stress began to be unbearable for Michael. In 1995 he was prescribed Prozac. The following year Paula Yates divorced Bob Geldof and also gave birth to Michael's daughter, Heavenly Hiraani Tiger Lily Hutchence.

1997 was INXS's 20th anniversary and it was decided to celebrate by organising a three-month Australian tour. Michael Hutchence arrived in Sydney on 18 November and lodged in room 524 of the Ritz Carlton Hotel, registered as Mr. Murray River. Paula Yates, Tiger Lily and Pixie and Peaches Geldof could not come as Geldof had refused to let them go because they couldn't afford to miss so much school. Legal proceedings were in progress to decide whether the girls could go to

Australia for at least the Christmas holiday. Michael Hutchence desperately wanted his daughter to be with him, since he hadn't seen her for four months, and he was upset by the fact that, in the eyes of the media and the public, he seemed to have been the one who had ruined a family. At 7.30 pm, on 21 November 1997, Michael had supper with his father. He had talked about his problems but he did not seem to be depressed. At 11.00 pm his former girlfriend, Kym Wilson, and her new boyfriend, Andrew Rayment, came to see him. They found him at the hotel with two women. They were the last people to see him alive. Michael said that he wanted to go to his room to check for news from London. Meanwhile he had received a call from his manager Martha Troup who had a business proposition for him, which they would discuss when she arrived in Sydney. Michael, Kym and Andrew had drinks and talked about his acting career. According to them, Michael seemed anxious and frustrated but not desperate. He told them this would be his last INXS tour. At 4.30 am Michael telephoned London, but the line was busy. At 4.40 am he phoned his friend Nick Cave. A little before 5.00 am Kym and Andrew left. They exchanged phone numbers and told him to call them if he needed anything. At 5.00 am a women sleeping in the next room was awakened by loud cries. Paula had called to tell him that the child custody hearing had been postponed until 17 December and that she did not want to leave England until then. Michael was devastated. A few minutes later he phoned Bob Geldof. It was a painful conversation. Bob explained that the decision had been made by the court and not him. Bob Geldof tried to calm him down and

THE EXPRESS ON SUNDAY 75P

NOVEMBER 23, 1997

WHY JOHN MAJOR WILL LOOK AFTER DIANA'S BOYS

Full Story • Page 5

PAULA LOVER IN SEX DEATH

TRAGIC COUPLE: Hutchence and Paula planned to marry next year

ROCK STAR Michael Hutchence's death may have been caused by a bizarre sex game that went wrong, the investigators said last night.

The 37-year-old INXS lead singer was found hanging from a leather belt attached to a door in his Sydney hotel suite. Police at first indicated he had killed himself. But there was no suicide

FROM FRANK THORNE IN SYDNEY

note and fellow guests drinking with Hutchence in the Ritz-Carlton hotel bar hours before he died said he had been happy and relaxed. His former lover Paula Yates was told of his death at her **TURN TO PAGE 2, COLUMN 2**

MARY KENNY ● **THE QUEEN WILL NEVER CHANGE • PAGE 17**

213 top Michael Hutchence formed INXS in Sydney in 1977. The name was suggested by the manager of Midnight Oil, Gary Morris, as a tribute to British band XTC and a brand of Australian marmalade IXL. But it also means "in excess."

213 bottom 23 November 1997: the front page of *The Express* reports the death of Michael Hutchence.

214 6 November 1990: Michael Hutchence on stage at the Frankfurt Festhalle during the promotional tour for the band's seventh album, *X*.

215 The INXS during a 1997 concert.

explain the situation, even suggesting that they meet. Michael hung up the phone.

At 6.00 am he called a former girlfriend, Michelle Bennett, leaving her a voice message. He had seemed to be drunk. At 9.40 am he called Martha Troupe in her office but she did not answer. He left a message, saying that he had had enough. At 9.54 am Michelle woke up and called him back. Michael told her he was exhausted and wasn't able to sleep. He didn't know how he would be able to go to the INXS rehearsal session, the last one before the band began its tour. He broke down in tears. Michelle told him to wait for her and that she would arrive at the hotel shortly. She brought a book with her, since she had often managed to help Michael to sleep by reading to him. Michael left his last message at the hotel reception desk. It was for the tour manager Jon Martin, informing him that

he would not be taking part in the rehearsal that day. Michelle knocked at the door of his room at 10.40 am There was no response. She tried to phone the room, but Michael did not answer, so Michelle thought that he had perhaps managed to fall asleep after all and left him a message under the door with her cell phone number. Then she went to a café to wait for a call, which never arrived. At 11.50 am a maid went into room 524 to do the cleaning. Michael Hutchence was kneeling on the floor, naked. He had tied his belt around the automatic door closure and had hanged himself. In the room the police found bottles of alcohol, traces of cocaine, many medicine bottles and an open phial of Prozac in the bathroom. The police report stated that he had committed suicide. But was this true?

Paula Yates raised a doubt: Michael was a

debauchee and liked to experiment with extreme erotic games, including autoerotic asphyxiation. His death was considered accidental. According to Yates, Michael would never have abandoned her and Tiger Lily. However, none of the witnesses and physicians involved in the investigation corroborated this hypothesis: in his condition he would not have indulged in an erotic game. No one knows what really happened in room 524.

Yates, the Suicide Blonde, died on 17 September 2000. She stated that Michael Hutchence was her life and there was no reason to go on living without him. She was found dead at her house in Notting Hill, London. Alcohol, medicine and heroin were found in her room. Was it an accidental overdose or suicide? Another mystery. After her death Bob Geldof requested and obtained custody of the young Tiger Lily.

COZY
POWELL

[19 December 1947 > 5 April 1998]

Cozy Powell holds a record for having played the greatest number of drums in less than a minute, a feat he achieved on BBC television's *Record Breakers*. That was the best example of his frenetic way of interpreting the role of drummer and of his powerful, rapid style. The problem was that Cozy Powell did everything the same way, without ever stopping. Above all, when he was in an automobile.

Colin Flooks was born in Cirencester, England in 1947 and when he was only 15 he adopted the stage name Cozy Powell and played in a local band called the Corals. Although he was so young he had already created a spectacular drum solo. That was the beginning of a great career as a session drummer, during which he played with all the leading names of British rock. His first important work (after a series of sessions with The Sorcerers, The Ace Kefford Stand and Big Bertha, as well as an appearance at the Isle of Wight festival with Tony Joe White) was in 1970 when he became the drummer with the Jeff Beck Group, with whom he cut two albums, *Rough and Ready* and *Jeff Beck Group*. But, what impressed the rock public most was his first single as a soloist on the instrumental *Dance with the Devil,* which got to number three in the UK singles charts in 1973. From that time on Cozy Powell constantly looked for bands to play with and became one of the most highly respected and sought-after instrumentalists on the British rock scene. After playing for two years with a band of his own, Cozy Powell's Hammer, in 1975 he joined Rainbow, led by Ritchie Blackmore, with which he recorded five albums and inaugurated the first edition of the Monsters of Rock Festival at Castle Donington, on 16 August 1980, with a headlining set. For the whole of the 1980s Cozy Powell continued to change bands. He played with the Michael Schenker Group, with Whitesnake, with Keith Emerson and Greg Lake in the Emerson, Lake & Powell band (a pop rock revival of the Emerson, Lake & Palmer progressive trio) and also with Black Sabbath. Then he joined Brian May of Queen, who had just formed the new Brian May Band, for two solo albums, *Back to the Light* and *Another World,* and also went with him on the promotional tour, in which the band supported Guns N' Roses, in 1993. He then played with Peter Green, formerly of Fleetwood Mac on the Peter Green Splinter Group albums. His final recording was the single of Colin Blunstone's *The Light Inside.* As the keyboardist Jon Lord, of Deep Purple, once said: "Playing with Cozy Powell is like a kick in the ass for every musician." The list of leading rock bands he played with was almost infinite, as were his desire to play and his urge to drive as fast as possible. On 15 April 1998, Cozy Powell was dashing down the M4 motorway near Bristol, in his Saab 9000. He had just finished recording his fourth solo album, *Especially for You,* and was about to go on tour with Brian May. But he was speeding and had not fastened his seatbelt. Furthermore, he had been drinking and was speaking to his girlfriend on a cell phone – a series of fatal mistakes. His car went out of control and overturned, killing him instantly. After having played on more than 66 albums during his life, not to mention posthumous releases, one of the best British rock drummers had ended his race.

216-217 Cozy Powell with Rainbow in 1976. The drummer played with Ritchie Blackmore's Rainbow from 1975 to 1980. His last concert was at the first Monsters of Rock Festival at Castle Donnington on 16 August 1980.

218 Cozy Powell posing in front of Graham Hill's car at the Zandvoort raceway in Holland, in 1974. "I drive a car the same way I play drums: like a madman."

Daily Mail, Tuesday, April 7, 1998

Page 30

THE HEAVY METAL STAR WHO SAID: 'I DRIVE LIKE I DRUM ...MADLY'

Rock drummer Powell dies in car crash

By KATE GINN

SEVENTIES rocker Cozy Powell has been killed in a car crash.

The 59-year-old drummer died when his car smashed into barriers on the M4 near Bristol, it emerged last night.

Powell had a passion for fast cars and motorbikes, and a love of speed.

He once told an interviewer: 'I drive like I drum – madly.'

The career of Cozy Powell – real name Colin – reads like a roll call of many of the biggest rock bands of the era.

He was a member of Rainbow, Black Sabbath, Whitesnake and Emerson, Lake & Powell. He also appeared with Donovan, The Who's Roger Daltrey, Gary Moore and Brian May of Queen.

In 1973, Powell had a number three chart solo hit with Dance With The Devil. He recently made a comeback playing with Peter Green, founder of Fleetwood Mac.

From the age of 14, Powell rode motorbikes, often in races. He later switched to cars, saying 'they're a bit safer' and competed in saloon car championships, turning professional for a year.

'When I get in a car, all I can think of is getting to that chequered flag first,' he said.

The man who admitted 'getting kicks from living dangerously' once insured his body for £1million after a series of stunts, including jumping a motorbike over his drum kit.

Six years ago he suffered minor injuries when his racehorse Pin collapsed and died on top of him, pinning him against a car.

Powell, who lived in Berkshire, was married but split up with his wife Madeline. The couple did not have any children.

His musical career began in 1965 as a member of The Sorcerers. By 1971 he had established his reputation as one of the country's leading drummers. He formed his own band, Bedlam, then joined Rainbow for four albums before moving on to Black Sabbath and Whitesnake.

By the Nineties he was playing with and producing Black Sabbath. In 1991, he turned up on Comic Relief's number one single The Stonk with comedians Hale & Pace.

Other solo hits included The Man In Black and Na Na Na.

Record producer Mickie Most led the tributes last night, praising Powell's musical skills and his great character.

'He was one of the best drummers we've ever had in this country,' he said.

'He was a great guy and a fantastic musician.

'Like me he loved fast cars and motorcycles, but unfortunately maybe he loved them too much.'

Cozy Powell: Switched from motorbikes to cars because 'they're a bit safer'

219 top and bottom Cozy Powell played on over 70 albums and with all of the leading musicians of English rock. When his Saab 9000 crashed on the M4 motorway he had just finished recording his fourth solo album, *Especially For You.*

LAYNE

STALEY

[**22 April 1967 > 5 April 2002**]

Layne Staley, who hailed from Kirkland in the cold and rain swept state of Washington, was a fine example of how rock 'n' roll might be the child of suffering. His story was marked by angst and suffering that was handed down through two generations and that found an outlet in music but resulted in the death of a young man. Ruined families, and that anxiety described by Douglas Coupland in his book *Generation X*, created the grunge aesthetic and sentiment in that Pacific Northwest state. Grunge was a musical style that had taken rock to its most basic level and had dominated the 1990s, but it had also ignited a flame that flared briefly and took the lives of many talented young musicians.

Layne Staley felt he had been doomed to darkness. The pain he had carried since his early childhood had been almost overwhelming. His father, Phil Staley, had left the family home when Layne had been only seven years old. His mother remarried and, for a while, Layne Staley became Layne Elmer after his stepfather Jim Elmer. He was told that his father had died, but he hadn't and, later, Layne found out that father was an alcoholic and a heroin addict. Layne vented all angst in his music. He had begun to play drums at the age of 12 and had then decided to become a singer. He worked at the Music Bank rehearsal studios in Seattle and lived in an abandoned recording studio with his friend Jerry Cantrell, with whom he formed his band, Alice in Chains, in 1987. The other members of the band were drummer Sean Kinney and bassist Mike Starr. Alice in Chains exploded onto the grunge scene and immediately enjoyed success: their first album *Facelift* (1990) sold two million copies in the United States, while the second album, *Dirt*, debuted as number six in the charts and was awarded quadruple platinum certification in 1992. "It was at this point that my father decided to return after 15 years," Layne related in his biography, *Angry Chair*. "He had seen my photo in a magazine. He told me he had been clean of drugs

for six years. So why in the hell didn't he come back before?" It had been yet another lie. Their meeting triggered an incredible self-destructive spiral: Layne was trying to kick his habit, but his father went to Layne to get high, and the two began to shoot up heroin together. Despite the huge success of *Dirt* in the charts, Alice in Chains did not go on tour to promote the album, and Mike Starr left the band, being replaced by Mike Inez. Layne Staley was in free fall but, nevertheless, continued to create great music. In 1994 Alice in Chains released their second acoustic EP, *Jar of Flies*, which debuted at number one in the charts, making it the first Alice in Chains release and the first EP to do so. The following year saw the release of *Alice in Chains*, which had been written almost entirely by Layne and went on to sell another 2 million copies; it also debuted at number one in the charts. But Layne was not able to go on tour because of his addiction problems and a bout of depression that had been aggravated by the news of the death, in October 1996, of his former fiancée Demri Lara Parrott: "They [drugs] worked for me for years," he said in an interview in *Rolling Stone*, "and now they're turning against me – and now I'm walking through hell." His final years were an abyss of solitude and suffering.

In 1999 Layne isolated himself completely, spending months without seeing or contacting anyone. Sean Kinney called him regularly three times a week, but Staley never answered; Sean spent hours screaming in front of Layne's door, but his friend never opened it. Every once in a while Layne would go to the Rainbow, a bar near his condo. He wouldn't order anything to drink, but would just sit at a small table, in silence. His friends left him alone for increasingly long periods, and then he died, alone. On 19 April 2002 his mother Nancy McCullum received a phone call from his accountants telling her that there had been no withdrawals from his bank account for two weeks.

221 Layne Staley in 1990, about the time when the debut album by Alice in Chains, *Facelift*, was released. In 1994 and 1995 the band released straight to number one in the American charts twice in a row with *Jar of Flies* and *Alice in Chains*.

222 Layne Staley singing live on 7 July 1991. On the following page, the *New York Times* relates how the vitality of this artist was suffocated by his drug addiction.

223 Alice in Chains: Mike Starr, Jerry Cantrell, Layne Staley and Shawn Kinney.

"WHEN THE SUFFERING UNDOES THE ARTIST"

[The New York Times]

She called the police and two policemen broke down the door of his apartment in the University District. What they saw was chilling: Layne had been dead for about two weeks. He was lying on the couch, the TV was still on, empty spray-paint cans were scattered about, and on the small table were two crack pipes and a small stash of cocaine. He had been killed by speedball, a mixture of cocaine and heroin.

A terrible end. In solitude – at least until the time the VH1 TV channel broadcast an interview with Mike Starr, the first Alice in Chains bassist, on the *Celebrity Rehab* program. Mike was the last person to see Layne alive, on 4 April 2002. Layne had been in a terrible state but hadn't wanted Mike to call an ambulance. They argued over it and Mike Starr left. The last words he heard from Layne were: "Not like this. Don't leave like this." The following day Layne had died. Mike Starr never forgave himself for not having called an ambulance to save his friend. He himself died from an accidental overdose of prescribed medication on 8 March 2011.

224 Dee Dee Ramone's real name was Douglas Colvin. He was the most prolific composer of the Ramones and continued to write songs for the band even after he left it in 1989. His best-known signature song is *53rd and 3rd*, the second single from the Ramones' debut album, *Ramones*.

DEE DEE
RAMONE

[18 September 1951
> 5 June 2002]

Arturo Vega is a Mexican artist who was born in Chihuahua. He discovered rock 'n' roll when he was eight years old while playing with a radio. That had been in 1955, when he happened to hear an Elvis Presley song on a Texas station. From that moment he had begun to travel, following that sound. He went to San Francisco during the Summer of Love, then in 1967 to Monterey to see Jimi Hendrix, and in 1971 he arrived in New York. He had looked for an apartment in the Lower East Side and found a loft at the corner of the Bowery and 2nd. It had once been a plastic flower factory and Arturo turned it into his studio. One day a boy named Douglas Colvin came through the door, which was always open: "He had come to see a friend on the upper floor: He came in and said 'Hi, I like the music you're listening to'." That boy would later become famous as Dee Dee Ramone.

That had been around the time of the beginning of punk, a genre and social phenomenon that started in New York and went on to conquer the world. Arturo Vega's loft became the headquarters of Dee Dee Ramone's band, The Ramones, and the starting point of a revolution made up of black leather jackets, bizarre hairdos and songs that lasted only two minutes but were marked by unheard-of fury. Vega later recalled that the Ramones had come from a dangerous and destitute world and that they had played what they were able to play, with two pluses: speed and intensity. Vega went on to state that punk had been a response to the vanity into which rock music had lapsed during the 1970s and that it had brought rock back to its revolutionary origins, becoming the voice of a new generation that had been much more disillusioned and angry than the preceding one.

Douglas Colvin's father had been an American soldier and his mother was German, and he had spent his childhood in a military base in Berlin. Both his parents were violent alcoholics and divorced when Douglas was 15. His dangerous drug addiction began early; while still very young he would steal objects from the military base warehouses and exchange gas masks (which he also collected), helmets and old weapons for all sorts of drugs, especially morphine. His father sent him to a military school in Munich, but after the divorce his mother took Douglas and his sister, Beverly, to New York. They had lived in Forest Hills, in Queens. It was there that Dee Dee met John Cummings and Thomas Erdelyi, who played in a band called The Tangerine Puppets, and the vocalist of the glam rock band Sniper, Jeffry Hyman, who became Johnny, Tommy and Joey Ramone respectively. According to Joey Ramone, Forest Hills was a middle-class neighbourhood full of rich and snobby people and their snot-nosed children who were always whining. Those youngsters were everywhere and were unbearable, raising hell and then getting off scot-free, so that one got the urge to kill them, Joey related. It was at that time that they wrote the song *Judy is a Punk*. The Ramones' punk rebellion had begun in Forest Hills, moved on to Arturo Vega's loft (Joey and Dee Dee even moved in with the Mexican artist) and took shape on the stage of Manhattan's Performance Studios, where the band played its first concert on 30 March 1974.

It had been Dee Dee who had the idea of having all the members take the name Ramone, which came from a pseudonym used by Paul McCartney – Paul Ramon – when checking in to hotels on tour with the Beatles in the early days. After the Performance Studios, the Ramones began playing at the CBGB (Country, BlueGrass and Blues), a music club at 315 Bowery, founded by Hilly Kristal which, thanks to the Ramones, became the "birthplace" of punk. The band played there 74 times from August to the end of 1974 (the shows lasted only 20 minutes on average), and the following year, on the table in Arturo Vega's loft, they signed their first recording contract, with Sire Records. Arturo drew the legendary band logo, drawing inspiration from the U.S. president's official seal, and from to 1976 to 1977 the Ramones released three fundamental albums of American punk: *Ramones, Leave Home* and *Rocket to Russia*. That began a story that continued for another 11 albums, from *Road to Ruin* (1977) through *End of the Century* (1980), recorded in collaboration with Phil Spector and up to *¡Adios Amigos!* (1995).

Dee Dee Ramone played the bass guitar until 1989 and wrote many of the band's songs, becoming the symbol of the dark soul that made the pop punk sound of the Ramones so desperate and utterly realistic. And with the "one, two, three, four" he shouted to mark the tempo of every song they played on stage, he created a powerful and tragic icon. Dee Dee was the idol of Sid Vicious of the Sex Pistols, the rival of Johnny Thunders in the nihilist race to the punk throne and like them, he ruined and ended his life with unresolved drug problems. His biography *Poison Heart: Surviving the Ramones* is the hyperrealist diary of a lost soul behind the rock star myth, a rebel without any more causes who struggled every day with his addiction to heroin.

Dee Dee Ramone left the band in 1989 after recording *Brain Drain* and was replaced by C.J. Ramone: "I couldn't stand any more, I was exasperated," he had said. Life had become only tours and albums for him, the Ramones had become rich but had never spent a dime and never had a day's vacation. Furthermore, he had become fed up with Johnny, who treated Dee Dee as if he was his mother. The happy Ramones family self-destructed due to personal rivalry and arguments, and Dee Dee embarked on a solo career that became more and more insane. In 1987, when still playing with the Ramones, he debuted as a rapper with the name Dee Dee King on the album *Standing in the Spotlight*, then went on to play with GG Allin's Murder Junkies and with The Chinese Dragons.

His most successful post-Ramones project was launched in Amsterdam in 1994: Dee Dee Ramone I.C.L.C. (Inter-Celestial Light Comune). The other members of the band were Dutch drummer Danny Arnold Lommen and New York City bass guitarist John Carco, whom Dee Dee had met at an Alcoholics Anonymous meeting. On 17 April 1994 the I.C.L.C. released the album *I Hate Freaks Like You* (in which Nina Hagen also performed) and then left for a ten-month tour of 22 countries. After a gig in Argentina, while looking for his guitar, which had been lost or stolen, Dee Dee met and later married 16 year-old Barbara Zampini, a great fan of the Ramones. After I.C.L.C. disbanded, Dee Dee went back to play with the Ramones (he wrote *Born to Die in Berlin*, the last song

on the *¡Adios Amigos!* album) and also participated in their final show, at The Palace in Los Angeles on 6 August 1996, after which he formed a cover band of the Ramones called The Ramainz together with his wife Barbara (who played the bass) and drummer Marky Ramone.

The final years of his life were a hectic, frenetic race. Dee Dee released two more solo albums (*Zonked!* (1996) and *Hop Around* (2000)), pursued a career as an actor (he had a big role in the film *Bikini Bandits*) and as an artist, and had tours with the Dee Dee Ramone Band. Barbara Zampini remained by his side until the end. On 18 March 2002 Dee Dee went on stage, with the Ramones, at the Rock and Roll Hall of Fame: Johnny thanked the fans and

President George W. Bush, Tommy spoke of Joey who had died the year before, Marky spoke of Tommy's influence on his drumming technique. And Dee Dee thanked himself. This was the last prank of the cursed punk hero, who had turned 50 and thought he had made it. But it wasn't to be. On 5 June 2002 Barbara found him dead in their Hollywood home. The cause had been an overdose of heroin. The long love story of Douglas Colvin and drugs, to which he dedicated his crudest and most profound song, *Chinese Rocks*, ended in the only possible way. Dee Dee was to have performed in a final show at the Ventura Theater in Los Angeles. Carved on the lower part of his tombstone, in the Hollywood Forever Cemetery, is the following: "OK... I gotta go now."

227 Dee Dee Ramone on stage at the CBGB club in New York, where American punk was born. The Ramones played there for the first time on 16 August 1974.

ELLIOTT SMITH

[6 August 1969 > 21 October 2003]

On his 34th birthday Elliott Smith had decided to do without certain things: alcohol, caffeine, red meat, refined sugar, and above all, psychotropics, which he had been consuming in large quantities to cure his depression and his addiction to drugs. His final years had been quite difficult. He had showed evident signs of paranoia, had told everyone that he was being followed by a white van and that people working for his label, DreamWorks, had broken into his house to steal his songs. He smoked a lot of crack and heroin and had no longer been able to perform live. On 2 May 2002, during a concert with the band Wilco, at Northwestern University, he had been on stage for an hour without being able to finish even one song. He had apologised to the audience, stating that his left hand had fallen asleep. A few months later he was arrested in Los Angeles, during a concert given by his friends in the band Flaming Lips. The police had mistaken him for a homeless person and had held him in jail for the night. Smith had even tried to break his drug habit by going to a rehab clinic, but he had been unable to complete the treatment program. However, on 6 August 2003 Elliott decided to put his life in order. He had been working on a new album, *From a Basement on the Hill*, and had re-established his credibility, as a live performer, with two sold out concerts at the Henry Fonda Theater in Hollywood. All of that might have been a sign of a breakthrough.

Things hadn't always been like this. Elliott Smith had made his album debut in 1994, *Roman Candle*, followed by *Elliott Smith* and *Either/Or*. While grunge music was in full swing, Elliott had written acoustic songs that were delicate, poetic and unforgettable. And he had achieved success. Gus Van Sant had asked him to compose part of the sound track for his movie *Good Will Hunting* and Elliott had written a piece entitled *Miss Misery*, which was later nominated for an Oscar as the best original song, and a nervous Elliott played it at the Oscar ceremony, wearing a white suit. The Oscar was awarded to *My Heart Will Go On* by Céline Dion from the *Titanic* sound track, but Smith had been pleased all the same. At that time he had also signed a contract with a major record studio, DreamWorks, which had guaranteed a much wider audience.

But something inside him went wrong. He had a bout of severe depression and had talked of suicide. During a trip in North Carolina he had driven into a ravine; fortunately, his car's fall had been checked by a tree. Then, for a while, he had found enough energy to compose once again. On 25 August 1998 his first album with DreamWorks, *XO*, had been released and went on to sell 400,000 copies. Elliott then contributed to the sound track of *American Beauty* with a cover

of the Beatles' *Because* and in 2000 he released *Figure 8*, which was acclaimed by the critics and made the UK charts. Things had definitely begun to look up. Then, suddenly, heroin reappeared on the scene, followed by bouts of severe paranoia, disastrous concerts and his arrest.

Yet, on his birthday, Elliott Smith had been certain that a new phase in his life had begun and he began work on his next album. Everything had seemed to be going well until 21 October 2003, when an ambulance was sent to a house on Lemonye Street, in the Echo Park area of Los Angeles. Elliott's fiancée Jennifer Chiba had been frightened to death. They had had an argument and she had locked herself in the bathroom. Then she had heard a scream and when she came out of the bathroom she had seen Elliott standing with a knife in his chest. She had pulled it out and he had fallen to the floor. He died in the Los Angeles County University Medical Center at 1.36 am. On the table in his house was a note he had written: "I'm so sorry. Love, Elliott. God forgive me." The autopsy found no evidence of alcohol or illegal substances in his system, but there had been traces of prescribed anti-depressants. The case remains open: the police never officially declared his death to be suicide. Yet the mystery does nothing at all to cancel the loss of a silent hero, one of the most delicate and talented figures in 1990s rock music.

229 During the peak of grunge, Elliott Smith enjoyed success with five albums consisting of delicate acoustic songs: "'Depressing' isn't a word I would use to describe my music. But there is some sadness in it – there has to be, so that the happiness in it will matter."

DIMEBAG
DARRELL

[20 August 1966
> 8 December 2004]

To die on the stage after having lived there with the utmost fury and passion: that was the fate of Darrell Lance Abbott, the legendary metal guitarist with Pantera. Darrell founded the band in 1981 with his brother Vinnie Paul, the band's drummer. He adopted the stage name Diamond Darrell, and in the 1980s he appeared on the American glam metal scene with a series of independent albums. A drastic change in style began in 1987, when vocalist Phil Anselmo joined the band. That was the period of thrash metal music and Pantera began to modify its sound with *Power Metal* (1988). "These magic clothes don't play music, we do," Vinnie Paul said. The transformation was completed in 1990, when the band was able to debut at Atco Records with *Cowboys from Hell* after being turned down dozens of times by the major record labels. By then glam metal and the 1980s belonged to the past: Pantera shouldered the entire metal genre and became one of the most important bands on the scene, together with such veteran bands as Metallica, Slayer, Anthrax and Megadeth. The difference now lay in Darrell's powerful and complex guitar playing, Vinnie's much faster drumming and the furious voice of Phil Anselmo, who mostly ignored the melodies and sang in a raspy hardcore manner, with a unique delivery that best interpreted the metal canons, especially in live shows. The change was consolidated with their second Atco album, *Vulgar Display of Power* (1992) and with *Far Beyond Driven* (1994), which debuted at number one in the American charts. That was the period when Darrell decided to change his stage name to Dimebag

Darrell. After four years of intensive touring that included Japan and South America, Pantera was the leading American metal band.

But at the precise moment that it attained the height of popularity the band began a process of self-destruction: two months after the release of *The Great Southern Trendkill* (1996) Anselmo almost died from a heroin overdose after a concert in Texas. He claimed he had begun to consume the drug to relieve the backache caused by the concerts. That excuse was too absurd to be true. It was the last straw and triggered the explosion of tension among the band members. Dimebag Darrell could not tolerate the dark side of Phil Anselmo, who in the meantime had distanced himself from the band and concentrated on various solo projects, so that Pantera was not able to record again until 2000, when it released *Reinventing the Steel*, which was in fact their last album. The members of Pantera played together for the last time on 28 August 2001 at the Beast Festival in Yokohama, Japan.

That was a terrible blow for Dimebag Darrell, but he was not the kind of person who gives up and he was ready to make a new start. In just one year he and his brother Vinnie formed Damageplan, a band that aimed at resuming the transformation of metal where they had left off with Pantera. The brothers stated they wanted to move forward and expand their potential to the utmost. Damageplan debuted in 2004 with *New Found Power*, which made the top 50 in the United States, and immediately went on tour. The rage

was the same, as was the desire to play. But Dimebag Darrell's career ended absurdly on 8 December 2004 in Columbus, Ohio.

He lost his life on the stage of a club called Alrosa Villa. In the audience was a man armed with a pistol: Nathan Gale, an army veteran who suffered from schizophrenia. He was convinced that Darrell was responsible for the end of his favourite band, Pantera, and that he had even stolen songs that Gale himself had written so he could play them with Damageplan. Gale suddenly made his way through the crowd and jumped onto the stage. He went up to Dimebag Darrell and shot him in the head three times, killing him on the spot. Jeff Thompson, the security chief of the club, flung himself at Gale, but Gale continued shooting, fifteen times. He killed Thompson, another employee of the club, Erin Halk, and a member of the audience, Nathan Bray, who had gone onto the stage to try to help Dimebag Darrell. The sound technician John Brooks tried to stop Nathan, but was shot three times and then held hostage. At that moment seven policemen came onto the scene. One of them, James Niggemeyer, entered from the backstage area behind Gale. John Brooks tried to free himself, thus distracting Gale, which allowed Niggemeyer to shoot him several times in the head. The assailant fell to the floor. He still had 35 bullets left to shoot. The toll of that insane night was four dead and 15 wounded. Dimebag Darrell died on stage while he was doing what he loved most, playing music. His remains now rest in the Moore Memorial Gardens Cemetery in Arlington, Texas.

231 Dimebag Darrell founded Pantera in 1981 with his brother Vinnie Paul. He released nine albums with the band, from *Metal Magic* (1983) to *Reinventing the Steel* (2000). In 2003 he formed Damageplan with Vinnie Paul, Pat Lachman and Bob Zilla.

232-233 Dimebag Darrell playing live with Pantera in 1997. His solo in *Floods* from the album *The Great Southern Trendkill* (1996) was ranked 15th of the all-time 100 best by *Guitar World* magazine.

233 top and bottom Right: Nathan Gale's driving license; on 8 December 2004 Gale fired fifteen shots during a Damageplan concert in Columbus, Ohio, killing Dimebag Darrell and three other people, as the title of *Spin Magazine* reports. Doctors intervened to aid one of the other 15 spectators who were wounded during the shooting.

"OHIO GUNMAN KILLS DIMEBAG DARRELL AND THREE OTHERS IN NIGHTCLUB SHOOTING SPREE"

[Spin Magazine]

OHIO DRIVER LICENSE 8002-026-19-01

BOB TAFT, GOVERNOR
Franklin R. Callender, Registrar BMV

NATHAN M GALE
111 1/2 E 5TH ST
MARYSVILLE, OH 43040

LICENSE NO.   S.S. NUMBER (optional)
RP526621

BIRTH DATE   ISSUE DATE
09/11/1979   09/23/2004
EXPIRES ON
09/11/2008

Sex   HT   WT   Hair   Eyes
M   6-05 255   BLN   HAZ
Endorse   Class Type Two Part
             D   R

Restr
B

234 Michael Jackson in 1993. During his fabulous career he won 13 Grammy Award and 13 of his singles topped the charts in the United States. *Thriller* (1982) sold 110 million copies, more than any other album in history. Through the Heal The World Foundation, Jackson donated over 300 million dollars to help underprivileged children.

MICHAEL JACKSON

[29 August 1958 > 25 June 2009]

The death of Michael Jackson on 25 June 2009 signalled the end of an era. The end of one show and the beginning of another. His funeral, at the LA Staples Center on 7 July 2009, was a live global TV media event (with 31 million viewers in the US alone). On 24 August the LA coroner declared that his death was a homicide and the reconstruction of his final hours became a mystery. Every facet of his life was put under the media's magnifying glass and subject to public scrutiny. The result – a portrait of a fragile man overwhelmed by the spectacle of his own life.

Michael Jackson was a child prodigy and grew to become the greatest and one of the most controversial stars in the world. His death, like his life, contained many obscurities. Who was the real Michael Jackson? He once said of himself that when you have lived in front of 100 million people since you were five years old, you become different.

His mystery began in Gary, Indiana, in 1963, where, as a game, five of the Jackson children formed a band. The family band began to take part in talent shows, first as "Ripple & Waves Plus Michael" and later as "The Jackson 5." Michael was the youngest and most talented member. Behind the band was a person who was disturbing, authoritarian and perhaps a criminal: their father Joseph Walter Jackson, known as "Joe," who was determined to exploit his children's talent to the utmost and by any means.

Michael Jackson's transformation into an entertainment machine began in the living room of the family living room, with severe discipline imposed by his father, whom Michael later called a genius, while at the same time recalling his violent ways: Michael's large nose, the way he sang, his stage presence – every trait of what was, after all, a small child, was judged and corrected by his father, sometimes violently. He withdrew into a shell, did not grow up and began to relate to the outside world through his talent. At around that time one Berry Gordy Jr., the boss of Motown Records, appeared. On 13 August 1967 the Jackson 5 won a competition at New York's Apollo Theater and were noticed by Gladys Knight, who got them an audition with Motown. When Gordy heard them sing James Brown's *I Got the Feelin'*, he knew he had struck gold and staked everything on them.

Michael's life became a pop fable: the discovery of the Jackson 5 was attributed to Diana Ross. Every move they made was planned to enthuse the public. Even Michael's age was manipulated. When their debut album, *Diana Ross Presents the Jackson Five*, was released, he was eleven, but the press was told that he was only seven. The first four singles, *I Want You Back, ABC, The Love You Saved* and *I'll Be There*, went to number one in the charts and they became one of the most perfect commercial products in the history of pop. In 1975 they severed their ties with Motown, followed the disco wave and released their two best albums, *Destiny* (1978) and *Triumph* (1980).

At that point the family band was already a

thing of the past as Michael had gone off to conquer the world on his own. While Madonna *interprets* her era, Michael Jackson *anticipated* his, adding elements that existed only in his imagination. "Michael had great imagination", said Quincy Jones, the third key figure in his life and the one who made him the world's greatest pop star. The two met on the set of *The Wiz* (1977) a musical remake of *The Wizard of Oz*. Their collaboration produced *Off the Wall* (1979) which went to number three in the charts earning Michael his first Grammy. Quincy Jones created an adult sound enhancing Michaels' dancing talent. The child prodigy had become a star.

But was he happy? That was the time when physical appearance changed mysteriously. Michael said he had broken his nose while dancing and had his first rhinoplasty. *Off The Wall* was a great success, but Michael was not satisfied.

That dissatisfaction led to *Thriller*, the best-selling album in history. Quincy Jones understood that times had changed and that disco was finished, and he wanted to take Michael into the sphere of rock. Thus was born *Beat It*, the single with an Eddie Van Halen solo. Michael toyed with mystery, with horror, with his own paranoia, and transformed it all into amazing songs. The *Thriller* video marked a turning point. Michael was the first African-American in heavy rotation on MTV and the *New York Times* commented that "in the world of pop music there is Michael Jackson and there is everybody else". On 25 March 1983, at Motown's 25th anniversary gala, Michael's transformation was fully achieved: he the moonwalk for the first time, a step that he

had learned three years earlier from Jeffrey Daniel, a *Soul Train* dancer. As ballet star Carla Fracci stated, in his dance steps the physical presence fades away into pure lightness and intangibility. Michael Jackson had become a moving image.

The 1980s marked his triumph, yet he became a prisoner of his own success. He had changed; he no longer transmitted that wonderful carefree sensation, which was disquieting. He still had a magic touch, so tangible in *We Are the World* and *Bad*. With Quincy he sought a sound that was more rock with a grittier approach and asked Martin Scorsese to shoot the *Bad* video in the New York subway. *Bad* was released on 31 August 1987 and debuted at number one in the charts. Michael returned to the stage with his Bad World Tour of 123 dates.

Then something went wrong. A mysterious illness, vitiligo, made his skin pale. Physicians became an oppressive presence in his life, which was marked by plastic surgery, anorexia and bizarre behaviour. Supposedly he had purchased the bones of the Elephant Man and was rumoured to sleep in a hyperbaric oxygen chamber. Although Elizabeth Taylor proclaimed him King of Pop, he became popularly known as Wacko Jacko.

He made his first comeback in 1991. He released *Dangerous*, performed 67 shows and amazed his public with his *Black or White* video. He was paler, he was stranger, but he was still Michael Jackson. It was the world around him that had changed. *Dangerous* topped the Billboard charts but was surpassed by Nirvana's *Nevermind*. The king was still on his feet and had that historic TV interview with Oprah Winfrey to an audience of 90 million viewers but then he fell.

Michael's child sex abuse trial began in 1993. It contained all the ingredients of a high drama: America's obsession with reality shows, the public's morbid curiosity, "unconventional" judges and lawyers, and unscrupulous witnesses seeking their moment of fame. Michael reached an agreement and made another comeback. He married Lisa Marie Presley, released *HIStory* and played an 82-show tour. But other mysteries cropped up: he and Lisa Marie divorced and he married Deborah Rowe, his dermatologist's nurse, and became the father of two children that were never seen by the public. The pop fable was a thing of the past and even the release of a new album triggered a long legal battle with Sony. The album was *Invincible*, which went to number one in the charts; but this had little effect, since there was no promotional tour and the singles from the album had not been carefully chosen.

In 2001 Michael celebrated 30 years as a solo performer with concerts at New York's Madison Square Garden. Then mystery once again clouded his life: a third child whose mother's identity was never disclosed, another trial for child sex abuse, financial problems and the closure of Neverland, and lastly his escape to Bahrain, where he was followed by a huge and ruthless media circus.

238 27 June 1999, Munich:
Michael Jackson and Slash
during one of the benefit
concerts of the "Michael
Jackson and Friends" tour.

239 15 September 1993:
Michael Jackson performing
at the Luzhniki Stadium in
Moscow during his
Dangerous World Tour.

Michael Jackson said he never regretted anything in his career, that it was both the most beautiful and the ugliest thing in his life, and that he was getting ready to make yet another comeback. He wanted to regain his status as a perfect entertainment machine. At that point the mystery of Michael Jackson became a tragedy. *This Is It* was the name of the comeback tour that originally called for ten dates in London's O_2 Arena but soon became 50, from 13 July 2009 to 6 March 2010, a feat that played havoc with an already weak body. Michael rehearsed at the Staples Center in Los Angeles with choreographer Kenny Ortega and rented a house at 100 North Carolwood Drive, Holmby Hills, Los Angeles. That was the address that an ambulance sped to at midday on 25 June 2009. Michael had had a cardiac arrest and died a few hours later in hospital. What really occurred during his final hours? Who was Conrad Murray, his personal physician? The county coroner stated that Murray had given him an injection of Propofol, a powerful anaesthetic used in operating theatres, to help him sleep. That was what stopped Michael's heart beating, as it was already very weak due to excessive consumption of psychotropic drugs and sedatives.

Michael Jackson did not manage to return to the only place where he felt truly free – the stage. The world lost one of its most brilliant talents, whose death only deepened the mystery of his life.

Los Angeles Times

75¢ DESIGNATED AREAS HIGHER © 2009 96 PAGES WST

latimes.com

King of Pop is dead at 50

Michael Jackson is stricken on the eve of a comeback tour

OBITUARY

A major talent, a bizarre persona

He dazzled the world with his music, baffled it with his behavior.

GEOFF BOUCHER
AND ELAINE WOO

Michael Jackson was fascinated by celebrity tragedy. He had a statue of Marilyn Monroe in his home and studied the sad Hollywood exile of Charlie Chaplin. He married the daughter of Elvis Presley.

Jackson met his own untimely death Thursday at age 50, and more than any of those past icons, he left a complicated legacy. As a child star, he was so talented he seemed lit from within; as a middle-aged man, he was viewed as something akin to a visiting alien who, like Tinkerbell, would cease to exist if the applause ever stopped.

It was impossible in the early 1980s to imagine the surreal final chapters of Jackson's life. In that decade, he became the world's most popular entertainer thanks to a series of hit records — "Beat It," "Billie Jean," "Thriller" — and dazzling music videos. Perhaps the best dancer of his generation, he created his own iconography: the single shiny glove, the Moonwalk, the signature red jacket and the Neverland Ranch.

In recent years, he inspired fascination for reasons that had nothing to do with music. Years of plastic surgery had made his face a bizarre landscape. He was deeply in debt and had lost his way as a musician. He had not toured since 1997 or released new songs since 2001. Instead of music videos, the images of Jackson beamed around the world were
[See Persona, Page A12]

1958 - 2009
Michael Jackson performs in Taipei, Taiwan, in 1996 during his "HIStory" tour. At the time of his death he was in Los Angeles rehearsing for an upcoming series of 50 sold-out shows at London's O2 Arena.

SIMON KWONG Reuters

HARRIET RYAN, CHRIS LEE,
ANDREW BLANKSTEIN
AND SCOTT GOLD

Michael Jackson, an incomparable figure in music, dance and culture whose ever-changing face graced the covers of albums that sold more than half a billion copies, died Thursday, shortly after going into cardiac arrest at his rented Holmby Hills mansion. He was 50. He spent much of his life as one of the most famous people on the planet, and to many, his untimely death felt both unthinkable and, oddly, inevitable.

Paramedics found Jackson in cardiac arrest when they arrived at his home shortly before 12:30 p.m., three minutes and 17 seconds after receiving a 911 call. His personal physician was already in the house performing CPR. Jackson was not breathing, and it appears he never regained consciousness. Paramedics treated Jackson at the house for 42 minutes, and he was declared dead at 2:26 p.m. at UCLA Medical Center, about two miles from his home above Sunset Boulevard.

"I got to kiss him and tell him goodbye," said Frank DiLeo, Jackson's manager and friend of 30 years, who was at the hospital. "I lost a very dear friend, someone who I admired, someone who was the greatest talent I ever met or worked with."

Los Angeles police said detectives would launch a thorough investigation of the death. They cautioned, however, that they did not believe Jackson was the victim of foul play and that the investigation was standard after the death of a person with his level of fame. Authorities said they would examine whether Jackson had been taking medications that contributed to his death; an autopsy is expected to be performed today.

Jackson's death was confirmed outside the hospital by his brother Jermaine, who once performed alongside Michael as a member of the Jackson 5, a family act that began in the steel mill town of Gary, Ind., before making it big in the music industry.

Jackson — who most famously lived in Santa Barbara County at his Neverland Ranch, named for the island where Peter Pan and the Lost Boys were in no danger of growing up — had taken up residence in a seven-bedroom estate in Holmby Hills, which he was renting for $100,000 a
[See Jackson, Page A11]

A performer who tore down boundaries
Throughout his career, transformation was the great source of Jackson's art. And it was his biggest burden. PAGE A15

He was the king of style too
He understood the power of costume on and off the stage, and his idiosyncratic fashion sense influenced a generation. PAGE A14

Fans, paparazzi flock to hospital, homes
They block streets and blast the superstar's music as they wait for news or a glimpse of his famous family. PAGE A14

240 On 26 June 2009 the *Los Angeles Times* announced the news of Michael Jackson's death.

241 July 2009. A grief-stricken Queen Latifah speaks during Michael Jackson's funeral at the Staples Center in Los Angeles.

242 and 243 Michael Jackson fans pay homage to him with poems and gigantic murals placed outside the Staples Center in Los Angeles. The King of Pop's death was brought about by cardiac arrest, as the *Daily Mirror* reported on 26 June 2009. In November 2011 Jackson's personal physician, Conrad Murray, was found guilty of involuntary manslaughter and sentenced to four years imprisonment.

He was greatly appreciated by other musicians but never enjoyed much commercial success. Mark Linkous was Sparklehorse, a bit folk and a bit psychedelic, a band that from 1995 released four albums that became a benchmark for the American independent music scene, especially *It's a Wonderful Life* (2001). But, before that he had also been the guitarist of Dancing Hoods, a band that gave him his first success.

Mark Linkous was born in Virginia. Many members of his family had been miners, a fact that influenced his decision to study music and avoid spending his life working in a mine. He had lived in Arlington until he was 18, when he got on a bus and left Virginia heading to New York. In New York he co-founded Dancing Hoods, which released two albums, *12 Jealous Roses* (1985) and *Hallelujah Anyway* (1988), after which Dancing Hoods moved to Los Angeles. But, after having achieved no success there, they disbanded in 1989. Mark then returned to Virginia, retiring to his home, to write songs and to perform live every so often with The Johnson Family and Salt Chunk Mary. Those bands led to the formation of Sparklehorse in 1995. Mark wrote the songs and the band recorded them at his farm in Bremo Bluff, Virginia. Sparklehorse became a means of giving vent to the mysterious depression that was overwhelming him and that he had been trying to overcome with alcohol, anti-depressants and heroin. His problems started leading him to his doom as early as 1996, soon after the release of the band's first album, *Vivadixiesubmarinetransmissionplot*. Later that year, Sparklehorse opened for Radiohead in London. They enjoyed success with American college radio and were highly respected by Radiohead. Everything seemed to be going well for the new

band. But one night, Mark passed out in his hotel room due to an overdose of Valium, alcohol and anti-depressants. He lay on the bathroom floor for 14 hours, in such a contorted position, that his legs, which had been bent under his body, were seriously injured. A series of operations at Saint Mary's Hospital in London saved his legs, but he was wheelchair-bound for six months afterwards. Yet, despite the fact that his legs never fully recovered, Mark resumed his musical career with *Good Morning Spider* (1998), which contained a song dedicated to the hospital, *St. Mary*.

In 2001 things began to look brighter: he no longer recorded by himself in his Virginia farm, but worked with PJ Harvey, Vic Chesnutt and the great Tom Waits on a new album, which became *It's a Wonderful Life* (2001). Mark later admitted that he had had to drink five shots of whisky before could get up enough courage to call Waits. The two drove to California together and Waits contributed to the song *Dog Door*. Only two years had passed since the near-fatal overdose in London and Mark had regained his will to live, even though he wrote such lines as "I'm full of bees that died at sea."

MARK LINKOUS

[9 September 1962 > 6 March 2010]

It's a Wonderful Life was an album with delicate melodies and harmonies, a means of seeking hope in the world, of embracing life and at the same time of accepting depression and solitude. But those latter two afflictions continued to plague Mark, and it took him a further five years to record Sparklehorse's next album, *Dreamt for Light Years in the Belly of a Mountain* (2006): "I stopped working for so long that I couldn't pay the rent," he said. "I had some stuff written that I didn't put on the last album, so I saved all these little pop songs."

His next project was much more ambitious: a gallery of music and images that he realised with producer Danger Mouse and film director David Lynch: Lynch had taken 100 photographs that were to be the subject of a book published with the album *Dark Night of the Soul* (2009), which featured the best talents of American indie, including Julian Casablancas, Suzanne Vega, Black Francis of the Pixies, James Mercer of the Shins and many others. While at work on the album, Linkous collaborated with Christian Fennesz on the EP *In The Fishtank 15*. But *Dark Night of The Soul* remains the Sparklehorse testament, an album of pure musical poetry, the last desperate attempt of a fragile soul to cling to life. On 6 March 2010, Mark Linkous had been staying with friends in Knoxville, Tennessee. He had told them he was going out for a walk and had gone out the back door. He then sat in the street, and pointed a rifle at his chest. Only one shot, to the heart, killed him instantly. He had been 47. He had left no suicide note or farewell message. Nobody really knows what killed Mark Linkous. His family wrote to the Sparklehorse fan club: "May his journey be peaceful, happy and free. There's a heaven and there's a star for you."

PAUL
GRAY

[8 April 1972 > 24 May 2010]

There are two ways to go about understanding Slipknot. The first is to attend one of their concerts and experience the power and great aggression with which these nine young men, wearing masks, assault the public. The second is to go to the state of Iowa, in the American Midwest, and see the city where the band was formed and where it developed: Des Moines, a cultural desert. Vocalist Corey Taylor stated this quite clearly: "There's nothing else to know about Slipknot: we started from Des Moines and arrived on the stage. It's a straight line, all our life lies between these two extremes." Since Halloween of 1996, when Slipknot's debut album, *Mate.Feed.Kill.Repeat*, was released, everyone has asked, at least once, what kind of place Des Moines must be to have given birth to such a disturbing band. Des Moines has a population of about 200,000 people, 90 per cent of whom are white; it seems to be the national capital of insurance companies and is the location of the Iowa Caucus, the first truly important primary during presidential elections. Another important fact is that Ronald Reagan lived there for years, working as a disc jockey on a local radio station. Corey Taylor once described Des Moines as a terribly boring city. During their childhood it was an enormous, desolate agglomerate of old-fashioned conformists where every kind of young persons' activity was immediately put down: a city of old people, full of churches and bars that made you want to scream.

Paul Gray was born in Los Angeles but had grown up in Des Moines. He formed Slipknot, with Shawn Crahan and Joey Jordison, in 1995. The band merged the theatrical elements of shock rock with influences of nu metal, immediately amazing the public with their image: the band members wore monstrous Halloween masks and referred to themselves by numbers from 0 to 9. Their first demo attracted the attention of Roadrunner Records, which signed a contract with the band and released their debut album *Slipknot* (1999). The American public was astonished and immediately became passionate over Slipknot's obscure world, which attracted a solid base of fans concert after concert.

Corey Taylor explained to journalists that wearing masks was an extreme means of expressing everything they had inside themselves. He stated that the masks were a representation of the dark side that we each have inside us, and that by showing it one became a monster but then learned to become acquainted with that negativity, free oneself of it and become a better person. Unfortunately that solution did not seem to work for Paul Gray, as during his career with Slipknot he had become swallowed up, so to speak, by his stage persona, The Pig. Already, by 2003, following the release of the band's second album *Iowa* (2001), he had been arrested for drug possession, following a car accident. The mask had not covered or ameliorated his dark side.

The band's career continued with *Vol. 3: (The Subliminal Verses)* (2004) and *All Hope Is Gone* (2008), after which band members devoted their time to working on solo projects while waiting to return to the recording studio to celebrate the tenth anniversary of their first album. Paul was planning to collaborate with band called Hail! but on 24 May 2010 his career suddenly came to an end. The Slipknot bassist was found dead in room 431 of the Towneplace Suites Hotel in Urbandale, Iowa. The cause was an accidental overdose of morphine. For some time Paul had been struggling against drug abuse and had gone to rehabilitation centres many times. In an interview he had described how difficult it was not to fall back into drug dependence during tours because pushers were always hanging around, but the imminent birth of his son was giving him new strength.

"HE'S GOING TO BE SADLY MISSED, AND THE WORLD IS GOING TO BE A DIFFERENT PLACE WITHOUT HIM."

[Shawn Crahan]

248 and 249 Slipknot in Des Moines, Iowa, on 27 June 2008.

250-251 25 May 2010: Slipknot vocalist Corey Taylor during a press conference the day after Paul Gray's death. On that occasion Shawn Crahan declared: "The world is going to be a different place without him."

SCOTT COLUMBUS

129 decibels. That was the volume registered by Manowar in 1984, the loudest band in the world. That record was certified by the Guinness Book of World Records. Manowar is maximum heavy metal, music that the band considers to be the most glorious art form that has ever existed. Manowar love to beat world records. Apart from the loudness record, which they have since exceeded on two occasions, they also hold the record for the longest ever heavy metal concert, which took place on 5 July 2008 at the Kaliakra Rock Fest (now called the Kavarna Rock Fest) in Bulgaria. The concert lasted five hours and one minute and comprised over 40 songs. At the drums during that performance had been Scott Columbus, seated behind his so-called Drums of Doom, a kit made of stainless steel, because he played so violently that he ruined all other types of drum sets. For that matter Scott became the Manowar drummer after having been discovered, by a fan of the band, while he had been working in a foundry.

Manowar began in 1980, when bassist Joey De Maio met guitarist Ross "The Boss" Friedman. Joey had been working as a roadie for Black Sabbath during their Heaven and Hell tour, while Ross had been one of the founders of one of New York's cult punk bands, The Dictators. The vocal lead was Eric Adams and the drummer was Carl Canedy, who, later, was to be replaced by Donnie Hamzik neither of whom managed to survive the stress of playing in Manowar. The band debuted in 1981 with *Battle Hymns* (on which Orson Welles narrated *Dark Avenger*) and went on their first tour. They needed Scott Columbus, who made his debut on *Into Glory Ride* (1983). Since then Manowar has had several line-up changes (for example, Joey De Maio fired Ross the Boss in 1989, who was replaced by David Shankle and he, later, by Karl Logan) and have released 9 further albums, from *Hail to England* to *Battle Hymns MMXI*, bombarding the metal public with songs that are enmeshed with Norse mythology, fantasy legends and battles between warrior divinities.

Scott Columbus had been seated behind his Drums of Doom until 1991 and then again from 1993 until 2008. But a mystery had begun to appear in his life. No one knows why, at a certain point, he decided to leave the band the first time, choosing his own replacement, Rhino. It was rumoured that his son had been ill – but Scott, later, flatly denied this in an interview – or that he himself had become ill. He didn't even explain the reason why he eventually stopped altogether, in 2008: "I had a long and wonderful career with Manowar. I have no regrets; it's just life moves on." Scott Columbus simply went below the radar until 5 April 2011 when an official communication from Manowar announced that he had died. He had been 54. The cause of his death remains unknown.

253 Scott Columbus during a photo session in 1984. The drummer played with Manowar on *Into Glory Ride* (1983), *Hail to England* (1984), *Sign of The Hammer* (1984), *Fighting the World* (1987), *Kings of Metal* (1988), *Louder Than Hell* (1996), *Warriors of the World* (2002) and *Gods of War* (2007).

AMY WINEHOUSE

According to what people say, she did the wrong things. She drank a lot and either ate too much or not at all. She had so much talent that success, and the public's great enthusiasm over her voice, seemed only natural to her. Amy Winehouse said "enough" too early, or perhaps it was the right moment after all. One day in late July, when the temperature was 104°.

Amy Jade Winehouse was born on 14 September 1983 to a Jewish family that lived in Enfield, in that part of England one never sees on TV. Her family was like so many others, with a grandmother, Cynthia, who was a rarity. In fact, Amy wanted to be buried near her grandmother. From her father, a taxi driver, she absorbed the stories of those who travel without looking out the window, and from her mother, a nurse, the suffering in hospitals – doctors and silence without an answer. As a child Amy already had the voice of a person who had something to say. Her first guitar arrived just after her last doll and, in between, she was expelled from school for having her nose pierced. She needed someone who really cared for her, but this means finding the right person. "Love is a losing game," she later sang. In 2003, when she was 20, her first album, *Frank*, was released. Only two more albums (one of which, *Lioness: Hidden Treasures*, was released posthumously) were needed to make her an unforgettable star in the history of music, a comet destined to remain and to spawn followers who were not always her equal. And, indeed, the success of *Frank* (platinum certified for exceeding 300,000 sales) lay in her surprising "black" voice that was much more mature than was to be expected of a person her age. Her second album was a supernova, *Back To Black* (2006). In the UK it topped the charts in a few weeks, while it got to number seven in America. Here the music drew inspiration from the girl bands of the 1950s and 1960s and the album was produced by Salaam Remi (who had also produced *Frank*) and Mark Ronson. The first single, *Rehab*, released on 23 October 2006, was a sincere, ironic and disenchanted autobiographical confession of Amy's refusal to go to a rehab clinic for her alcoholism. The result was sensational: the song won five Grammy Awards, red carpets were rolled out everywhere for Amy and her face appeared on posters in all over the world. But her success had a dark side. Her life was marked by contrasts. She became extremely thin and then regained her former weight; she was violent, often drunk, consumed drugs and vomited in public and in clubs, in turn sweet and desperate, and began to sing again. That same year, 2007, she married Blake Fielder-Civil in Florida; they divorced two years later and this was the tormented love that destroyed her. And she was arrested in Norway for possession of seven grams of marijuana. In the meantime her fame grew exponentially helped by media gossip, violence, turbulent behaviour in public, and art. Her European tour, in the summer of 2011, began and ended disastrously: during the first date in Belgrade, she was in a state of utter confusion, or at best drunk, and was not able to sing. The tour was cancelled.

A few weeks later, on 23 July, she was found dead in her London home. It was the fate of a person who doesn't know what fate is. The examining physicians wrote that she died of drugs and alcohol, as well as from a form of shock called stop and go: heavy drinking after abstinence. But they were wrong. Stop and go was the shock that allowed her to live, without concealing the negative aspects. She would stagger helplessly on stage, but once the microphone was in her hand she was back in the groove and captivated the audience with her unique, desperate voice. She once said she was not completely right in the head, but that no woman was, showing she knew that perfection is the deformed mirror of presumptuous people. She was a comet that burned out too quickly and sadly she became another member of the 27 Club, artists who died when they were 27, such as Jimi Hendrix, Jim Morrison and Janis Joplin. All of them suffered from an existential malaise that was more powerful than their art.

255 Amy Jade Winehouse was born in London on 14 September 1983. Her debut album, *Frank* (2003), sold 3 million copies. The following album, *Back to Black* (2006), made her the only English artist to win five Grammy Awards.

256 and 256-257 23 July 2011: the day Amy Winehouse died, hundreds of fans gathered in front of her house in Camden Square to pay homage to her. Her death was caused by an overdose of alcohol and drugs. Her funeral took place on 26 July 2011 at the Edgwarebury Lane Cemetery in London.

258-259 and 259 Amy Winehouse performing in two concerts of her 2007 tour: on stage at the Coachella Festival in California (left) and at the Highline Ballroom in New York (right).

260-261 Amy Winehouse performing live during the Eden Sessions in the Eden Project in Cornwall. The singer once declared she was not totally right in the head, but that no woman was.

WHITNEY
HOUSTON

263 In 2009 the Guinness Book of World Records stated that Whitney Houston was the female performer with the most awards of all time. She released seven albums and three film soundtracks, and over 170 million copies of her albums were sold. With her second album, *Whitney* (1987), she became the first female artist to enter at number one in the American charts, in 1987.

[9 August 1963 > 11 February 2012]

A bodyguard found her soul as well. It continued to be helpless, exposed to the winds of uncertainty and to a life that is never what you want it to be, not even when it is the one you have dreamt of. Whitney Houston was always an octave above the others without having to sing loudly, the only one who really moved listeners even when she sang catchy melodies instead of songs. She was the good girl next door who mixed with the wrong crowd. And, at a certain point, she saw that the road leading back was too long and too dark to take. It all ended in a hotel room in Beverly Hills, like stars of yesteryear. A true star, a combination of talent and marketing. The American Dream without the anger. The African-American girl who made good without having to say that she was different in a country that forces you to be equal.

Whitney Elizabeth Houston was born in Newark on 9 August 1963. Like so many African-American girls she began singing at a very early age, in the choir of the New Hope Baptist Church – the same one where her friends and admirers would later bid her farewell. She then leapt from gospel music to global music, singing everything: soul, rock and country. There was no lack of good music in her family. Her mother, Cissy, sang with Sweet Inspirations and her cousins were Dionne and Dee Dee Warwick. Whitney was not only a fine singer and a good girl but beautiful too, the girl everyone would like to marry. Success was inevitable for her, as a singer, actress and model. Her image appeared on the covers of glamour magazines and she acted in movies. But her eyes were those of a person who always feels out of place, too talented to think that she had talent, too demanding of herself, afraid of having too much too soon. Hollywood brought her the success of *The Bodyguard*, a movie that remained in the heart of her co-star, Kevin Costner, who became a true supporter and mentor for Whitney in front the camera, an actress who lacked the great talent of those who really know how to act. And Costner returned to "have a talk" with her at her funeral, betraying feelings that went beyond those of a person who had merely shared a movie set with her for a few weeks. *I Will Always Love You*, from the movie's soundtrack, sold 42 million

copies. Then she made the touching film *The Preacher's Wife*, with Denzel Washington, and there the box office showed that she was quite capable of making good choices and of changing. She sang with the greatest and it was the stars who wanted to perform with her.

Her problems began at home. Her marriage to singer Bobby Brown (from 1992 until 2006) was opposed by everybody. He was violent and became more so, seemingly, with every passing day. She had entered a cul-de-sac and never quite managed to get out: drugs and alcohol. She looked skinny and distracted, her voice came and went, she had problems remembering lyrics. Then Whitney tried to start all over again, but new problems arrived to accompany the old ones: anorexia and bulimia. She was still a star and people still loved her, but there was more compassion than encouragement in their feelings towards her. So that was really the end because when you have no more enemies you count for little and rehab clinics and detox programs will have no effect.

When the curtain came down Whitney had just finished a new movie. But the musical *Sparkle* was destined to be released posthumously. She was found dead on 11 February 2012, at the age of 48, in the Beverly Hilton Hotel in Beverly Hills, where she was expected to participate that very evening in a Grammy Awards party. A mixture of drugs and alcohol made her faint in the bathtub of her hotel room and she drowned. When a bodyguard arrived her condition was already hopeless and she died a few seconds later.

Whitney died, but not her music, not the affection people had for this fine African-American girl who had lost her way. That was made clear at her funeral, which was celebrated on 18 February in the same Baptist church in Newark where it had all started. Time stood still in America. In the church were 1,500 people, including Kevin Costner, Aretha Franklin, Elton John, Jesse Jackson, Alicia Keys, Stevie Wonder, Mariah Carey, Beyoncé and Oprah Winfrey. And the words of the "bodyguard" Costner moved everyone: "Off you go, Whitney. Off you go. Escorted by an army of angels and your heavenly father. When you sing before him don't you worry, you'll be good enough."

264 Whitney Houston performing in 1990, at the peak of her career.

264-265 5 May 1988: Whitney Houston singing at the Wembley Arena in London. Her verve, grit and talent earned her the title of Queen of Pop, which was used by the *New York Post* on the occasion of her death.

"QUEEN OF POP DEAD"

[New York Post]

266-267 15 February 2012, a fan writes a message in memory of Whitney Houston on a huge commemorative poster placed in a shopping precinct in Manila, Philippines.

267 top Whitney Houston's funeral was held on 18 February 2012 at the New Hope Baptist Church in Newark, New Jersey. Various artists, including Stevie Wonder, Alicia Keys and R. Kelly, took part in the ceremony.

267 bottom Whitney Houston was buried in the Fairview Cemetery at Westfield, New Jersey, next to her father John Russell Houston, who died in 2003.

INDEX

c = caption
bold typeface = chapter

PHOTO CREDITS

Richard E. Aaron/Redferns/Getty images: pages 100, 103
Alpha/Globe Photos/ZUMAPRESS.com: page 205
Mario Anzuoni/Reuters/Contrasto: page 242 top
AP Photo/LaPresse: pages 46, 91 top, 123 bottom, 140-141, 233 center
John Atashian/Corbis: page 206
John Atashian/London Features/LFI/Photoshot: page 222
Roberta Bayley/Redferns/Getty Images: page 226
Bentley Archive/Popperfoto/Getty Images: page 74
Bettmann/Corbis: pages 27, 50-51, 189
Joel Brodsky/Corbis: pages 53, 58, 59
Steve Brown/RetnaPictures/Photoshot: pages 248, 249
Marc Bryan-Brown/Corbis: page 215
Bob Campbell/San Francisco Chrolicls/Corbis: page 82
Ric Carter/Alamy/Milestone Media: page 63
CBS Photo Archive/Getty Images: page 13
Central Press/Getty Images: page 120
Jacques M. Chenet/Corbis: page 176
Stephanie Chernikowski/Michael Ochs Archive/Getty Images: page 227
Cinetext/Tips Images: pages 26, 48, 194-195
Collezione Privata: page 185
Tom Copi/Michael Ochs Archive/Getty Images: page 163
David Corio/Redferns/Getty Images: pages 160-161, 264-265
Fin Costello/Redferns/Getty Images: pages 106-107, 143, 154-155, 216-217, 219 top, 253
Kevin Cummins/Getty Images: page 111
James D. DeCamp/Columbus Dispatch/AP Photo/LaPresse: page 233 bottom
Ian Dickson/Redferns/Getty Images: page 115 top
Henry Diltz/Corbis: page 146
Volker Dornberger/dpa/Corbis: pages 236-237, 238
Franck Driggs Collection/Archive Photos/Getty Images: page 64
Bill Ellman/Mirrorpix: page 34 top
Estate of Keith Morris/Getty Images: page 77
Deborah Feingold/Corbis: page 173
Tony Frank/Sygma/Corbis: page 25
John Frost Newspapers: pages 15 bottom, 34 bottom, 42, 72, 81 bottom, 86, 102 top, 115 bottom, 122, 123 top, 141, 147 bottom, 150 bottom, 191 bottom, 195 top, 213 bottom, 219 bottom, 240
Grant Goddard/Getty Images: page 87
Lynn Goldsmith/Corbis: pages 209, 213 top
Tim Hall/Redferns/Getty Images: page 60
Gijsbert Hanekroot/Redferns/Getty Images: pages 188, 218
Larry Hulst/Michael Ochs Archives/Getty Images: pages 181
Hulton Archive/Getty Images: pages 124-125
Anwar Hussein/Hulton Archive/Getty Images: page 97
Mick Hutson/Redferns/Getty Images: pages 199, 232-233
Steve Jennings/Retna Limited, USA/Photoshot: page 229
Robert Johnson Estate/Hulton Archive/Getty Images: page 11
Ivan Keeman/Redferns/Getty Images: pages 32, 75
Mike Kemp/In Pictures/Corbis: pages 256-257
Bill Kennedy/Mirrorpix: pages 130-131
Keystone-France/Gamma-Keystone/Getty Images: pages 30-31
Junko Kimura/Getty Images pages 126-127
Ian Kingsnorth/Alamy/Milestones Media: page 260
Daniel Lainé/Corbis: page 129
Elliott Landy/Magnum Photos/Contrasto: page 39
Justin Lane/epa/Corbis: page 267 bottom
Charles Langella/Corbis: pages 244-245
Francois Le Diascorn/Gamma-Rapho/Getty Images: page 55
Wang Lei/Xinhua Press/Corbis: page 267 center
Luke MacGregor/Reuters/Contrasto: page 256
Mike Maloney/Mirrorpix: page 102 bottom
Karen Mason Blair/Corbis: pages 174-175
Stan Mays/Mirrorpix: page 33
Clay Patrick McBride/Getty Images: page 231
Richard McCaffrey/Michael Ochs Archive/Getty Images: pages 136-137
Jim McCrary/Redferns/Getty Images: pages 69, 71
Lennox McLendon/AP Photo/LaPresse: page 150 top
Gary Merrin/Globe Photos/ZUMAPRESS.com: page 187
Franck Micelotta/Getty Images: pages 202-203
Mirrorpix: pages 35, 94 bottom, 203, 242 bottom
David Montgomery/Getty Images: page 37
Chris Morphet/Redferns/Getty Images: page 93
Philip Morris/Rex Features/Olycom: page 105
Tim Mosenfelder/Getty Images: pages 208
Tony Mottram/Retna Ltd./Photoshot: pages 153, 178-179
MPTV/LFI/Photoshot: page 84
MPTVA/LFI-HA/Photoshot: page 81 top
Bernd Muller/Redferns/Getty Images: pages 214
Michael Nagle/The New York Times/Redux/Contrasto: page 259
Charlie Neibergall/AP Photo/LaPresse: pages 250-251
NY Daily News Archive/Getty Images: page 124
Michael Ochs Archives/Corbis: page 147 top
Michael Ochs Archives/Getty Images: pages 15 top, 19, 20, 20-21, 23, 38, 40-41, 43, 44, 45, 47, 49, 56, 57, 65, 73, 83, 94 top, 117, 120-121, 145, 157, 165
Denis O'Regan/Corbis: pages 191 top, 224
Denis O'Regan/Getty Images: pages 192-193, 197, 258-259
Harry Page/Mirrorpix: page 195 bottom
Anastasia Pantsios/LFI/Photoshot: pages 182-183
Rene Perez/AP Photo/LaPresse: page 164
Jan Persson/Redferns/Getty Images: page 79
Pool New/Reuters/Contrasto: page 241
Neal Preston/Corbis: pages 90, 96, 114, 132, 134-135,149, 150-151, 234-235
Neal Preston/Retna Pictures/Photoshot: page 91 bottom
Mike Prior/Redferns/Getty Images: pages 132-133
Michael Putland/Retna/Photoshot: pages 66-67, 89, 113
Romeo Ranoco/Reuters/Contrasto: pages 266-27
RB/Redferns/Getty Images: page 29
RDA/Rue des Archives: page 169
David Redferns/Redferns/Getty Images: pages 159, 167, 180
Ebet Roberts/Redferns/Getty Images: pages 99, 171
Jack Robinson/Hulton Archive/Getty Images: page 95
Richard Sharman/Retna Pictures/Photoshot: page 246
Max Scheler-K&K/Redferns/Getty Images: page 119
V. Siddell/Retna/Photoshot: page 211
Paul Slattery/Retna/Photoshot: page 101
Ted Soqui/Corbis: page 243
Stills/Retna UK/Photoshot: page 85
Marty Temme/WireImage/Getty Images: pages 221, 223
Greetsia Tent/WireImage/Getty Images: page 131
Ian Tilton/Camera Press/Contrasto: pages 200-201, 201
Time & Life Pictures/Getty Images: page 264
Rob Verhorst/Redferns/Getty Images: page 109
Juergen Vollmer/Redferns/Getty Images: page 17
Robert Wallis/Corbis: page 239
Walt Disney Films/Everett Collection/Contrasto: page 263
Donna Ward/Getty Images: page 255
Scott Weiner/Retna Ltd./Corbis: pages 138-139
Bob Willoughby/Redferns/Getty Images: page 168

AUTHOR

MICHELE PRIMI is a journalist and radio and TV author, works for *Rolling Stone* and writes for *Emergency*, *GQ Italia*, *Wired Italia* and *Riders*. Since 2007 he has written musical programs for Virgin Radio and Virgin TV; from 2000 to 2006 he wrote for MTV Italia, La7, Sky and The Family; since 2007 he has been a correspondent from Spain and in 2011 he was sent to New York as the correspondent for the daily *l'Unità*, *Rolling Stone* and Peacereporter.net. Primi has also published three music monographs on the band Queen for the Giunti Editore publishing house and also edited the texts of the photographic volume "Uno sguardo sul Burlesque" (A Glance at Burlesque) published by RCS Libri. For White Star he edited the appendix of the Italian edition of the volume "Legendary Rock Songs."

Cover and Back cover
A photo collage.
(© John Frost Newspapers)

METRO BOOKS
New York

An Imprint of Sterling Publishing
387 Park Avenue South
New York, NY 10016

This 2014 edition published by Metro Books, by arrangement with De Agostini Libri S.p.A.

Translation: Richard Pierce
Editing: Norman Gilligan

ISBN 978-1-4351-5191-8

For information about custom editions, special sales, and premium and corporate purchases, please contact Sterling Special Sales at 800-805-5489 or specialsales@sterlingpublishing.com.

Manufactured in China

2 4 6 8 10 9 7 5 3 1

www.sterlingpublishing.com